Sarah's Olympic J(
From
Tears to Cheers

CW00855404

By

Phil Thomas

2nd Edition

ISBN 978-1-291-11591-8

This book has not been written by a professional author, but by a loving parent, who has been on an incredible journey. I thought that by writing this book many others could experience the journey that we have been on.

We could not have completed this journey without the help of numerous people, some who I would like to thank now.

Linda Treharne, Sarah's 1st hockey coach and the person who first saw how talented she was.

Margaret Medlow, Sarah's 1st Welsh hockey coach, who nurtured and encouraged her to improve.

Alan Lints, performance director for the then, Welsh Hockey Union, who advised Sarah, that if she wanted to play for GB, she would have to go abroad to play high performance hockey.

Maria and Joanne, they have given Sarah, Sheila and I constant support for many years.
Nick and Zoe Lamb, whose friendship and support have been second to none throughout.
Emma, Bisham Abbey's physiotherapist, for the work and dedication on getting Sarah fit in time for the 2012 Olympics

And finally the most important person, who I suppose made all of this possible and who has been by my side every step of the way, Sheila, Sarah's mother.

Thanks to everyone, because without you, we could not have done it.

Foreword:

This is the story of Great Britain and Wales, International hockey star Sarah Thomas. Sarah is now a double Olympian, and also won a Bronze medal in the London 2012 Olympics.
Sarah is extremely proud of being Welsh and of her Welsh roots having been born in Aberdare and brought up in Merthyr Tydfil, South Wales.
Sarah's drive, determination and guts took her from playing field hockey in a local Merthyr Tydfil hockey club to competing in two Olympic Games, at Beijing in 2008, and at London 2012. Her journey was never an easy one, but a journey she was determined to complete.

Chapter 1

The story really starts in the Cathedral city
of Hereford, just over the border from
Wales. It was a very cold but bright day in
October 1994. Sarah was 13 years old,
and we were having a family day out
shopping.
As we were walking back towards the car
park we stopped outside a sports shop,
there was some whispered chat going on
between Sarah and her mother, Sheila,
then Sarah turned to me and said, "Dad
can I have a hockey stick?" my immediate
reply was, "what do you want a hockey
stick for?" which was quite obvious
really, "to play hockey".

 Sarah had always been the sporty type,
she had done some running, including a

mini marathon, running 4.2 miles around our home town of Merthyr Tydfil, which she finished, and won a medal for taking part. Then Sarah took up playing tennis, and she even played some Dragon rugby, where we watched as she picked the ball up at the half way line, and ran like hell to score a try, and not even the boys that were also playing could catch her.

The hockey stick was a different kettle of fish, because up until then I had never heard Sarah mention that she wanted to play hockey, but apparently a local ladies hockey club, Dowlais ladies, were looking for new members, and had invited Sarah to go training with them. So for the princely sum of £7.50, Sarah's first hockey stick was bought. I remember looking in the rear view mirror as we travelled back home, watching her as she held and admired her shiny new hockey stick.

The following Thursday night at seven o'clock, I took Sarah to her first training session. I would drop her off and then go back home for two hours until it was time to pick her up again. Back in the car I asked Sarah, how it had gone, she replied "it was great I really enjoyed it", but I must admit, that in the back of my mind I thought give it a few weeks and the hockey stick would be laid to rest with all the other sporting equipment that we had bought for her; how wrong I was.

About six weeks later, I had gone to pick Sarah up from her training session as usual but I was a little early so I walked to where the Astroturf pitch was. The training had finished and the group were walking towards me. The coach for Dowlais ladies was Linda Treharne. Linda had been playing, and been involved with hockey for a number of years. She approached me and said, "Could I have a word about Sarah", "I said, yes sure". Linda then said "you know your daughter is talented, don't you" I replied "no", because up until then I thought it was just another fad that Sarah had. Linda then explained that Sarah had a natural talent for hockey. Linda Treharne could not have been more right.

Chapter 2

The hockey training continued, and Sarah was invited to become a member of Dowlais ladies hockey club. Sarah was now 14 years old, and every Saturday during the playing season, Sheila, Sarah's mother and I would drive to wherever the team were playing, and stand in all kinds of weather watching the game. Sometimes, due to Sarah's age and inexperience she would not get on to play at all other times she might just play for ten minutes but Sarah persevered until she was playing full games and scoring many goals.

Sarah's natural playing ability had now been noticed by a number of people in the hockey fraternity, and steps had been taken for Sarah to take part in a number of trials. The first trial was to gain a place in the County team, made only more awkward, because the school that Sarah was attending did not have a hockey team. Miss David, the schools PE teacher hastily put a team together so that Sarah could play in the trials.

The trials took place at another local school, where Sarah's talent, although a little rough around the edges, stood out. One of the selectors, who shall remain nameless said of Sarah, "I don't think she has any talent" that person has really had to eat her words over the years.

The road to actually playing for your country is a long one, with many trials, county trials where teams from the different counties play each other. Players are then selected from each county to go into regional trials in Sarah's case she was in the South Wales region. You would then have the North Wales region, West Wales region, and East Wales region. This culminated into a very large two day trial, where all the regions met and played hockey against each other, all the while being watched by the main Wales under 16 selectors. These trials were tough, for girls of such a young age, each player battling to be selected, and once the trials are over, the agonising wait for the letter to say whether you were successful or not.

Sarah's letter duly arrived, and thankfully she had been one of the lucky ones, she had been selected to now go for trials to get into the Wales under sixteen squad. The journey was still a long one, but there was light at the end of the tunnel, and the dream of wearing the red hockey shirt for Wales was becoming a reality.

Margaret Medlow was the tough no nonsense coach for the Welsh under sixteen's squad, and knew what she was talking about, having played for Great Britain herself.

Margaret was respected both on and off the field, and all the squad looked up to her, her coaching ability was second to none. The trials and training continued for many months, and the object of the training was the Celtic cup being held in Milton Keynes, only sixteen players out of the twenty five that were in the trials would be selected for this tournament.

On the final training day, a Sunday, the twenty five girls were called together, to be told who had been selected, and who had not, and waiting outside were all the anxious parents, praying that their offspring would be one of the selected players.

It was very sad to see the players who had not been selected, in tears, their parents trying to console them, but they were young and determined, and they would be there to try again next year.

Waiting outside, we could tell from Sarah's face that she had been selected, it was such a proud moment for us, and we couldn't wait until the next weekend, when the Celtic cup tournament would begin, and we would see our daughter wearing the red hockey shirt of Wales for the first time.

Chapter 3

We will never forget that first game in Milton Keynes, the whistle blew, and the first ball of the match was hit, and made its way to Sarah, this was the first touch of the ball for her, would she freeze on this new stage, or would she play the role she had been training for, for many months, tears of joy ran down my face, as she picked the ball up on the end of her hockey stick, and ran towards the opposition goal, neatly passing the ball to one of her fellow players, who beat the goal keeper and put the ball into the net, Wales, went on to win 1.0.

Over the next few years, we watched as Sarah became even more skilled, playing countless matches for her beloved Welsh squad, and at a small town in mid Wales called Newtown, as captain of the under sixteen squad, she scored one of the fastest goals on record, from the blow of the whistle to the ball going past the keeper into the net, the time was just seventeen seconds.

Because of Sarah's immense talent, she has also been invited to play with the under eighteen squad, and also, still at the tender age of just fifteen she had been selected to play with the under twenty one squad, in another Celtic cup tournament being held in Scotland.

A few weeks before Sarah's sixteenth birthday, we started receiving phone calls from BBC Wales, asking if they could

come and film Sarah playing, and do some
interviews with her, we asked Sarah if it
was OK, and she agreed to take part, and
at the time we did not know the reason
why they wanted to film her in action.

It was on a Saturday, in a small town
called Caerphilly, where Dowlais ladies
were playing in one of their league
matches, we were there as usual, to cheer
the players on, there was a camera crew
from BBC Wales, and the producer came
to speak with my wife and myself, after
the introductions, he told us in confidence
why they were filming Sarah, Sarah had
been chosen as BBC Wales female junior
sports personality of the year.

This was a tremendous achievement for
one so young, but the amount of time that
she put into her sport. The training, the
fitness, it was thoroughly
deserved. The night that the show was
broadcast we will never forget, when
Sarah, dressed to perfection, walked down
onto the stage to receive her Carwyn
James award, from Wales rugby player
Jonathan Davies, the crowds cheered,

clapped and whistled, it was a very proud moment for Sarah's mother and I.

After the show had been recorded, there was an after show party, where we all mingled with the celebrities and sports stars that were there.
The next day, Sarah had telephone calls from all over the place, from radio stations, and from friends, congratulating her, and as usual she took it all in her stride.

Chapter 4

During this time of Sarah training for the Welsh squad, and playing for her club each weekend, she also had to contend with studying for her GCE exams at school. Again we were very proud when she passed all the exams she had taken, and Sarah now had plans to take her A level exams, and to go to University. Sarah studied Physical Education, Psychology, and History for her A levels, and she was very pleased when she gained an A star in both the PE exam and Psychology exam, and a B in the History exam, enough to get her a place in University, and after looking at a few Universities, she decided to go to Exeter University and study for a BSC in Sports Science.

Sarah was about to leave home for the next three years and study at Exeter, but before leaving she had another exam to contend with, her driving examination, Sarah had been taking driving lessons with a local driving school, and the instructor now told Sarah that she was ready to put in for her test, the only problem was that Sarah was leaving Merthyr for the next three years. I contacted the driving examination centre, and was told it would take at least one month for Sarah to take the driving test, unless I paid extra for an earlier test, and the only date they had was the Saturday, before the Monday when she left for University. I booked the date that they gave me, and before we knew it the test day had arrived. I remember that Saturday well, Sarah was to take her driving test, we had a leaving party arranged in the evening for family and friends, and Wales was experiencing one of the worse storms of the year, the rain was bouncing off the ground and the winds were extremely high, but again Sarah took it all in her usual stride. Sarah had a one hour driving lesson at 10 o'clock and then her test at 11 o'clock. I remember looking out of the window just after her test would have started, and thought to myself, rather her than me driving in this atrocious weather, and if I'm honest, I thought that Sarah would not pass her test, mainly due to the conditions she had to drive in. Sarah's mother had gone shopping for all we needed for the forth coming party that evening, so I waited at home for Sarah's return, it was an anxious moment when I saw the driving instructors car pull up outside returning Sarah after the test, they both got out of the car, and the instructor gave Sarah a hug, I thought, was that because she had passed, or because she had failed, Sarah waved the instructor off and came through the door, I looked at her face, and the face said she had failed, but Sarah jumped into the air, and said "I passed", we hugged each other, and I said well done, we had another thing to celebrate that night. Sheila arrived back home with the shopping, and I went to help carry the bags of goodies in, I put on a glum look, and Sheila said, "Sarah failed did she" I said, well, "Look at the weather" then Sarah came around the door and shouted I passed, I passed. That evening despite the continuing bad weather, all our family and friends turned up for the party to celebrate Sarah going to University, it was a great night and everyone enjoyed themselves, but it was also a little sad, because Sarah would see very little of her family and friends for the next three years. Monday morning arrived, and we were all a little subdued, packing the car with all the things Sarah would need for her stay at Exeter University. At last the car was packed, and we all got in, Sarah said her last goodbyes to the home she would see little of for the near future. About a mile down the road, I looked across at Sarah, who was crying bitterly. That day we drove to Exeter was a sad day for us all as a family, because we had never been apart, except for Sarah's hockey trips abroad, and leaving Sarah there was an extremely difficult time for Sheila and me.

I suppose we were luckier than most families, because Sarah had been given a Sports Scholarship, for her hockey playing abilities, and her stay in the halls of residence were paid for through that Scholarship, with a proviso that she played hockey for the University team, and by the second and third years of her stay at Exeter, the University hockey team played in both finals of the Universities hockey cup at Milton Keynes.

After three long years, Sarah's graduation day came along, and it was Cap and Gown day at the University, where she was presented with her degree certificate, she had gained a BSC in Sports Science. In the three years that Sarah had spent in Exeter we had noticed a change in her accent, from being as we say in Wales "proper Welsh" she now had more of an English accent, and she also had become friendly with a lot of hockey players playing in the English leagues, her transformation had begun.

It was now time to leave Exeter, and head back home once again to Wales. I had hired a transit van, to bring back all the belongings, Sarah had collected over three years at the University. Eventually the van was fully loaded, Sarah said her sad farewells to all the friends she had made over the three years, all promising to come and visit Sarah back home in Wales, and over the years we have seen quite a number of them visit us in Wales.

Chapter 5

Coming back to her home town of Merthyr Tydfil was a difficult time for Sarah, after being away for so long, she was now out of touch with the friends that she had, before going away, and also she now had to find a job.

Sarah applied for a position of Disability Sports Development Officer with the local borough council, and after quite a lengthy interview, was told that she had been successful, and was offered the position. This was a demanding position for Sarah but also very rewarding. Sarah's job was to start sports workshops and clubs for the disabled children of the borough, and also to involve the parents, and train the parents in the equipment that was used, as the equipment had to be modified due to the children's disabilities, and once the sports club had been set up, and Sarah was satisfied with the parents training, she handed the club over to the parents for them to run, but she was always there for backup and advice.

Because of her training commitments this job was suitable as Sarah could work flexi-hours, because at this time she was travelling back and forth to Sophia Gardens in Cardiff nearly every day, she would organise her days, so that she could work with the sports clubs in the mornings, and then drive down to Cardiff to do her training, which at this time, was not only hockey training, but building up muscle strength through weights training, and then drive back, and do a few hours in the evening with the parents at the sports clubs.

At this time, Sarah was having one to one hockey coaching with a man called Alan Lints, an ex Australian hockey player, who had been employed by the Welsh Hockey union as head of coaching and technical development.

Alan Lints recognised the fact that Sarah was good enough to be in the Great Britain squad for 2004 Olympics, and before long Sarah was involved with the GB squad, travelling back and forth now to Bisham Abbey in Buckinghamshire, where all the GB training took place.

Chapter 6

The training at Bisham Abbey was constant and really hard work, mainly because the standard of play required to play with the GB squad is a lot higher, than club or country hockey, but as usual Sarah stuck with it, and was selected to go to Canada with the GB squad.
I remember looking at Teletext to see what the scores were out in Canada, and in the first game that Sarah played she scored the winning goal, although at the

time I was at home alone, I was jumping around the lounge thumping the air with my fist, shouting fantastic, fantastic.

To play in the 2004 Olympic Games the GB squad had to qualify, this meant the squad had to travel to different countries, and play in tournaments, and they had to win, Sarah was chosen to go to Australia, to play a few tournaments out there. Australia was a country that she had always wanted to visit, and this was a golden opportunity for her, spending a month in the sun training and playing hockey.

On her return to the UK from Australia, Sheila and I drove up to Heathrow to welcome Sarah home, and on the drive back to South Wales, Sarah although tired after her long journey, excitedly told us all about her trip, how she thought she had played well, and trained hard, and the camaraderie, with the other GB players was great, and Sarah also said that she hoped she would be selected to play in the Olympic qualifiers, which were the next big tournaments.

It was a sad day when Sarah was told by the then GB coach, that although she had played well in Canada and Australia, she would not be taking Sarah to the Olympic qualifiers, because she did not have the experience, that some of the older GB players had, and to this day I believe that was a big mistake, because GB failed to qualify for the Olympics, and although Sarah may have not had the experience of some of the older players, she certainly had the skill and determination to have made a difference when it was needed. As an example of that, in one hockey tournament, playing for Wales in France, Sarah had been sent off the pitch for some infringement of the rules, and as Captain of the Welsh team, she knew that she had let her team down, because they were losing 2-1 to France, after ten minutes Sarah was allowed back onto the pitch, and with only five more minutes remaining of the game, Sarah was passed the ball, and started her run towards the opposition goal, it was a tremendous moment watching as three French players chased Sarah, but all failed to catch or stop her, as she beat the goal keeper, and slammed the ball high into the net of the goal, which gave Wales a well deserved 2-2 draw.

In the course of life, some people try and fail, saying, "well at least I tried", failing is not even in Sarah's vocabulary. The determination that I mentioned earlier, is what makes Sarah go on. She hadn't made it to the 2004 Olympics, which she was bitterly disappointed about, but as with all professionals, she just put it behind her, and got on with her playing and training. Whilst a lot of girls her age were out partying and enjoying their selves, Sarah would be out in all weathers, rain, snow, running up our local mountains, down the local gym and practising her hockey on any Astroturf she could find, she had a new determination, the 2008 Olympics, but this time, she would use a different tack.

Chapter 7

Alan Lints the Welsh technical director, was also annoyed that Sarah had not been chosen for the GB squad to go to the qualifiers, and made his feelings known to others in meetings with the GB selectors, but he also had another plan.

Alan suggested to Sarah, that she should go to New Zealand where he had a lot of contacts, and play for a club out there, where the standard of hockey was a lot higher than in Wales or England.
Sarah discussed the move to New Zealand with Sheila and myself, and I said it was a long way to go, leaving all your friends and family, going to a country where she wouldn't know anyone, and what if it all went wrong, after we discussed all the pros and cons, Sarah made the final decision, it was too far, and she did not want to leave all her family so far behind, New Zealand was off the menu.
Alan Lints was not put off by this, and explained to Sarah, that she had to play a much higher standard of hockey, if she was determined to play in an Olympic games. Alan made a few more enquires, and came up with a solution, Sarah would still have to move away from her family and friends, but this time it was not so far,

Alan also had a lot of hockey contacts in Holland, and he had spoken to some colleagues in Rotterdam, and they were very keen to meet Sarah.

Rotterdam hockey club is a fantastic hockey venue, 7 outfield Astroturf pitches, and the main grandstand pitch, where all the first team games are played. Sarah was to fly out on a Friday on an all expenses paid trip to meet the Rotterdam management and coaches. They gave Sarah a full tour of the club and facilities, and also gave her a short tour of Rotterdam.

Sunday is the day when both the men's team, and women's team play their league games, and on this weekend they were both playing at home so Sarah had the chance of watching the side that she would be playing for, if she decided to move to Holland.

In Britain, all hockey players will tell you that spectators are few and far between, in a normal league game you may get between 20- 40 people watching the game, and even in big tournaments, you would be lucky to see a hundred or so, at

Rotterdam Hockey Club, Sarah was
amazed to see at least 1500 spectators just
for an ordinary league game, the facilities
at the club were second to none, it had a
huge bar area, a restaurant, and huge
spectator seating on both sides of the
pitch. The club had 2000 playing
members ranging in age from 7 year olds
to 70 year olds.
Sarah was very impressed, and told the
management that she had almost made her
mind up to join the club, but first she
would go home, discuss it with her
parents, and let them know in a few days.

Chapter 8

Sarah arrived back home very excited
about the prospect of going to play for one
of the best hockey clubs in the world.
Sarah told us all about the club, and
showed the photos that she had taken of
the facilities; she then showed us the clubs
web site, where you could take a virtual
tour of the club, and we also were very
impressed.
That night we all discussed the pros and
cons of Sarah moving to Rotterdam, I said

wait until you see the contract that the club was going to send to her, before making the final decision. Sarah contacted the management about the contract, and they said that they would get it in the post ASAP.

The contract arrived, and after reading all of it including the small print, the decision was made, Sarah was going to Rotterdam. The basis of the contract was, that Sarah would live rent free in a house, with three other hockey players, would be paid a monthly wage, for all the games she played, a free use of a car, and they would also pay for all her flights back and fore to the UK, arrangements now had to be made for Sarah to make the move to Holland.

Within a few weeks the move to Rotterdam had been all sorted out.
The Rotterdam hockey team were coming over to the UK to play a few pre-season friendly's with Canterbury hockey club in Kent, and during these games Sarah was going to play for Rotterdam.
The car was loaded up with all that we could take for Sarah, because after the final game with Canterbury on the

Sunday, Sarah would leave with her new Dutch team mates for Rotterdam. Sarah's mum and I stayed in a hotel just outside of Canterbury, so that we could go and watch the two games that Sarah would play with her new club.

The first game was on the Saturday at 2.00pm, and we were both exited, waiting to see Sarah in her new Rotterdam kit of green and white sponsored by ABN AMRO. The teams came out onto the pitch, and there was a great cheer mainly from the home team spectators of which there were many.

As the game progressed Sheila and I were getting strange looks from the other spectators, as we were the only British people cheering for Rotterdam.

It took Sarah a little while to settle down on the pitch due to the different formations and styles of playing that the Dutch team were using, and also it was difficult for her, due to the Rotterdam players speaking Dutch during their calls for the ball etc.

The Rotterdam team were mainly a young team, whereas Canterbury had a much older and wiser side, and this lead to Canterbury scoring first, and by the end of the first half were winning 1-0. The start of the second half saw Rotterdam playing with much more style and vigour, and this followed with a superb goal from their centre forward, the score was now 1-1. Sarah was playing well, but didn't seem to be getting much of the ball probably due to the fact that she wasn't known by the Rotterdam players, and they were passing to faces they knew. With just about ten minutes of the game left to play Rotterdam made another break towards the Canterbury goal, and scored again, 2-1 to Rotterdam, there were no further goals during the game, so it was a good win for Rotterdam.

We spoke to Sarah after the game and she told us she had enjoyed it, but found it difficult when they shouted out " Links" to her, which in Dutch is to go left. Sarah was staying in the same hotel as the Dutch girls, so that she could get to know her new team mates, so Sheila and I said our goodbyes to her, saying that we would see Sarah the following day for the next game.

The game on the Sunday started at 11.00 am due to the fact that the Dutch team would be travelling back to Holland straight after the game.
This time it looked as if the Rotterdam team were really out to win, because in minutes of the game starting they had scored, the Canterbury side looked quite shocked at the speed of the young Dutch team, and the style in which they had scored, the Canterbury side tried in vain to put on more pressure, but it was the Dutch team that came back at them even more strongly and scored again, 2-0 to Rotterdam. Sheila and I were praying that Sarah would get a good ball to her, giving her a chance of proving herself to her Dutch team mates and scoring, and we weren't disappointed, a good ball crossed to her from the left, Sarah picked the ball up on the end of her stick, and ran towards the Canterbury goal, easily beating the two defenders who tried to tackle her, and striking the ball powerfully into the goal,

3-0 to Rotterdam, and the first of many goals for Sarah.

Now came the hard part for Sheila and I, saying goodbye to Sarah once again, it always seemed to Sheila and I that we were always waving Sarah off, to some place or another. So Sarah left Canterbury for Holland, with her new club team mates, not knowing where in Rotterdam she would be staying, not knowing anyone out there, and not knowing the language, it takes a lot of courage to do that, it's something that most people could never do, but Sarah had her dream, playing in an Olympic games, and a plan, and this was part of that plan.

Once again the journey home to Wales was quite subdued, knowing now that the house we all share would be quiet again, because as all parents know a child's bedroom is an active place, with music playing, probably the TV on at the same time, clothes all over the place, Sheila and I were going to miss that a great deal.

Chapter 9

Sarah was now living in a house in Rotterdam, with three other hockey players, one female hockey player, and two male hockey players, and they all played for Rotterdam hockey club.

The house was owned by one of the clubs sponsors, who allowed the players to live there rent free. Part of Sarah's contract was to coach a young Rotterdam club side, aged between 12 years and 15 years, and one of her first jobs at the club was to introduce herself to the young side she was to coach. They all told Sarah that they had not done to well in the previous season, and had come third from the bottom in the Dutch league, that they played in.

Sarah told them, that with her coaching them, and if they had the desire to learn and work hard at their hockey, they would come in the top three this season, and she did not let them down, and they did not let her down, because at the end of Sarah's first season with this young side, they had come top of their league. The parents of the young side she coached were ecstatic, and all congratulated Sarah on her achievement.

Sarah's week consisted of getting up in the morning, and cycling to the club, where she would be either training with her team mates, or coaching her young squad, her young side would play their league game on the Saturday, then on Sunday, Sarah would be playing either away against another Dutch team in the premier league, or playing home at the Rotterdam club. It was in fact as Sarah described to us 24 hour hockey, and it had started to get Sarah down.

Sheila and I flew out to Rotterdam for our first visit to see Sarah, about a month after she had left home. The whole trip had been organised by Rotterdam hockey club, they had booked us in to a first class hotel right in the centre of Rotterdam. We were met at the airport by the head coach of Rotterdam hockey club, and driven to our hotel. A little while later Sarah joined us, and after plenty of hugs and kisses, showed us around Rotterdam. Although it was the end of September the sun was out and it was pleasantly warm. Sheila and I were impressed by this multicultural city, there were numerous bars and restaurants,

and to the delight of Sheila many places to
shop, after a while the girls dropped me
off at a bar for a glass or two of wine,
whilst they carried on shopping. On their
return from shopping, Sarah asked where
would we like to go for lunch, I said we
will leave it to you, Sarah said, I will take
you to the Hotel New York, to get there
you had to take a water taxi from the
quayside to the hotel. The Hotel New
York was a fantastic place it looked like
the inside of an old fashioned sea going
liner; it had a wonderful atmosphere and
superb food.

Over the four days we had in Rotterdam,
Sarah showed us the sights of the city that
she had been to in her time there and all
were enjoyable, but the highlight of our
trip was to Rotterdam hockey club, where
Sheila and I were treated like VIP's. The
club has 7 all weather Astroturf outfield
pitches, where the 2000 or so club
members train and play their league
games and then there is the main stadium,
where the first team sides play. It was
twelve o'clock on a Sunday morning and
the place was packed with players who
had just finished their games, supporters

who were there to watch the first teams play their games, children in their playing gear, ready for their matches, it was really buzzing.

Sheila and I sat in the lounge overlooking the main Astroturf pitch, were at 12. 45 exactly we would watch Sarah play against Den Bosch, who were top of the league.

We were sitting quietly with a glass of wine each, when one of the parents of a first team player asked us why we were sitting there, I was a little confused, when she explained that all parents of the first team sat in the VIP lounge which was upstairs, we were shown the way to the upstairs lounge, and introduced to all the parents, who had come to support that day, and like most Dutch people they all spoke good English, and asked us how Sarah had come to play out in Holland. It was time for the game, and most of the parents stayed in the upstairs lounge to watch the game through the huge glass windows, but Sheila and I wanted to taste the atmosphere outside.

The stadium was full of Rotterdam's spectators and also a huge contingent of Den Bosch supporters.

Both the game and atmosphere were electric, and it was great to watch Sarah play again and with so much gusto. The score was 0-0 at half time, which was good because Rotterdam had always lost by a few goals to the Den Bosch side. It was also lovely to hear the Rotterdam supporters shout, Go Sarah Go, when she got the ball, and started one of her very impressionable runs; the Dutch had taken her into their hearts, and were very fond of her, after such a short time at the club. Den Bosch managed to score a goal towards the final minutes of the game from a short corner, and the crowd weren't happy, shouting at the umpires out there is par for the course.

So we left the club with Rotterdam having lost 1-0 to Den Bosch. Sarah was in high spirits, having enjoyed the game, and knowing that she had played well.

Sheila and I visited Sarah many times whilst she was living in Rotterdam, and we don't know if we were jinxed or not, but they never won one game that we watched, when Sarah told her Dutch team mates that her parents were coming out to visit, they all used to say, oh no, we are going to lose on Sunday.

Chapter 10

The hockey seasons out in Holland run from the beginning of September to the middle of December, then from February to the end of May. Out of season Sarah would fly back home, and spend as much time with us as possible. The training regime still carried on though, and also when Sarah wasn't playing for Rotterdam, she still had her playing commitments for Wales. Sarah was now captain of the Wales Senior women's squad, and had to lead by example, at this time Sarah was travelling back and forth to Cardiff almost every day, and one day a week she was travelling to Bath University for weight training. On the days that Sarah had to travel to Bath, I would go with her and do the driving to give Sarah a break, sometimes I would have to wait three hours or more, just sitting in the car reading a few daily papers, but it did take some of the pressure off her.

Wales Senior women's team had a Celtic Cup tournament ahead of them, and this year it was being held up in Wrexham, the teams involved were Wales, Ireland, Scotland and France. The training prior to the event was going well, although a few older more experienced players had dropped out of the squad, either through injury or other commitments, one of the squad, was actually getting married whilst the tournament was on.

For the tournament four of us parents had decided to drive up and stay the weekend in Wrexham, we thought we could watch the games have a few drinks with friends living in that area, whose daughters were playing in the Welsh squad. Our friends Dave and Jane Hopkins, whose daughter Carys, was one of the leading welsh players in the squad travelled in the car with Sheila and myself. The drive up to Wrexham on the Friday was uneventful, and quite pleasant, although for the past few weeks it hadn't stopped raining, and there was quite a bit of flooding about, we had to make a detour or two because of the flooding, but eventually arrived at our hotel in Wrexham.

The first game was on Saturday morning at 11 o'clock, Wales were playing against France, and so far the rain had held off, but just after half time, the rain started, and soon it was pouring down.
The game resumed for the second half, and Wales were beating France, 1.0. The Astroturf was covered in water which made playing the game very difficult for both sides; France tried again and again to breach the Wales defence but failed each time. About 10 minutes before the end of the game Wales managed to score another goal, 2.0 to Wales, France seemed to tire towards the end and never looked as if they would score, and the game ended with Wales the victors. I thought it was a great start to a tournament, and believed that Wales would do well, how wrong I was.

The next match was on Sunday at noon, Wales were to play Scotland, it had rained most of the night, but at the start of the game, again it was actually dry. About fifteen minutes into the game, the rain started again, the sky was black, there was thunder and lightning, both teams had great difficulty in playing and passing the ball, but it looked like Wales were struggling the most, they were losing 2-0 within ten minutes, and this time Wales didn't look as if they would score, Sarah did have a fine chance hitting the ball very hard at goal, but it was deflected over the net by the Scottish keeper. Half time came, and both teams were glad to get off the pitch, by now the rain was bucketing down, and in my opinion, the game should have been abandoned, but it wasn't, both teams came back out for the second half, and nobody looked as if they wanted to play hockey, I couldn't really blame them. Scotland scored another 2 goals in the second half, Scotland won 4-0.

The final match was Wales versus Ireland at 11o'clock on Monday morning. The Welsh squad had seemed to have dried out from the previous day's game, and started off well, passing the ball accurately and with style, both teams attacking and counter attacking right through the first half, but both being unlucky in actually scoring a goal, and so far it had stayed dry.

We had been told by others who had come to watch the game, that they had seen on the news that a lot of the country was flooded, and that we would have to take great care travelling back home. One of our main concerns was for some of the Welsh squad who had travelled to Wrexham in their own cars, and for their safety travelling back home.

The game resumed after half time and again Wales were playing strongly, attacking at every opportunity, but still unable to score. With just 15 minutes to go Ireland attacked strongly, and forced a penalty corner, the corner was taken, and the ball was hoisted neatly into the Welsh sides' goal 1-0 to Ireland with just 10 minutes to go. Wales gave one final push to try and equalise and with just a few minutes remaining, Wales also managed to get a penalty corner, the ball was pushed into the circle, the ball was stopped and the striker hit the ball with

great force into the Irish goal, a great
cheer went up from the home crowd, and
the game ended in a well deserved draw
for Wales 1-1.
We all left Wrexham a little subdued; it
had not been the best of tournaments for
Wales, and we put it down to the atrocious
weather conditions. For the majority of
the players for Wales that was the end of
their season, for Sarah another round of
trials and an immense amount of training
lay ahead, as she was again named in the
GB squad of around 30 players for the
2008 Beijing Olympics, but only 16 out of
the 30 players starting training would
actually go to the Olympics. There would
be another round of disappointment for
some; Sarah's mother and I were praying
that this time around, Sarah would achieve
her goal.

Chapter 11

The new hockey season was about to start
at Sarah's hockey club out in Rotterdam,
but this season they would only have
Sarah there to play just a few matches.
Danny Kerry the GB Women's head

hockey coach, had told all the players that they would be required to live as close to Bisham Abbey, where the National Sports Centre was, due to the intense amount of training involved in the run up to the Beijing Olympics.

The first game Sarah had with her club at Rotterdam was on the 15th of September 2007, she would play just one more game before returning home to her home town of Merthyr, and then Sarah would be travelling back and forth to Bisham Abbey, and also to the Welsh Institute of Sport in Cardiff.

The training at Bisham Abbey began in earnest, Sarah knew some of the players as she had been involved with them in previous GB squads, but there were a number of new players also. Sarah was required to drive up to Bisham on say a Monday, she would train for two or three days, staying in the sports accommodation at Bisham, and then drive home again for a few days, but in the days that she was at home, Sarah had to travel to Cardiff to do her weight training at the Welsh Institute of Sport with her personal trainer.

Danny Kerry the head coach made it clear to the players involved with the GB squad, that he would need them living close to Bisham Abbey very soon, as there were a few test matches coming up against Australia, at Bisham in November 2007, and then in December 2007, the GB squad would fly to Argentina for three test matches out there, and then in January 2008, the GB squad would fly to Australia for five test matches and four friendly games.

Sarah was now concerned, because she had nowhere to stay in the Bisham area, but she also knew that she had to move up there. The Welsh Hockey Union were making enquiries to see if they could find Sarah somewhere to live for the next nine months prior to the Olympics, but without success.
The other problem was the cost of moving to that area, the only income Sarah had was from the Sports Lottery fund of about £425 a month, this would have to cover

the cost of the accommodation, and her living expenses.

The English Hockey offices, based at Bisham Abbey were also trying to find suitable accommodation for Sarah, and also to try and find her some part time work to pay the bills. Where Sarah was going to find the time to do all the training and work as well was beyond me.

The Squad of thirty players was to be reduced to twenty six prior to the test matches against Australia in November, there were a few players with injuries, which were stopping them from fully committing themselves to the training, and it looked like these would be the first casualties of cutting the team down in size, although they were told that if they regained their fitness they could be recalled into the squad at any time, this kept the other players on their toes because no one wanted to be dropped from the GB squad.

Chapter 12

My wife Sheila and I had already decided to go and watch the matches against

Australia at Bisham Abbey, obviously hoping that Sarah would be involved, as the team to play had not been announced as yet. We had booked a hotel in High Wycombe which would be our base for the three days that we were there; the drive from the hotel to the hockey pitch was around twenty minutes, which was fine. In the mean time another team member had told Sarah, that there may be a place available to stay, it was on a farm close to Bisham Abbey, the owners had already had an athlete stay with them, but that person had now left, and they were deciding whether or not to take another athlete into their home, Sarah rang and told Sheila and I the news, she was exited and relieved that a place to stay may come up, but alas a few days later she rang again to say that the owners of the farm had decided not to take another athlete into their home. We had hit a brick wall; Sarah had no permanent place to stay, and not a great deal of money to look for a place to stay on her own. Then another opportunity raised its head, there was a cottage about eight miles away in a little village called Hambledon, the owner lived in Ireland and was renting the cottage out, the previous tenant had now left, and with the winter fast approaching the owner was very keen to get another tenant in, to keep the cottage warm and dry throughout the winter. Sarah approached another GB team member who was also looking for a place to rent, and together they went to view the cottage, again excitement grew, Sarah sent me pictures of the cottage, and it looked beautiful, it had a thatched roof, a lovely garden, and it was in a superb location, the only downfall was the rent, the owner wanted a£1000 a month. Sarah and her team mate tried some negotiation with the owner, who Sarah said seemed a very nice person, and in the end the owner said that she was prepared to reduce the rent, mainly because she needed someone in the property quite urgently, the owner was prepared to drop the rent to £900 per month. Sarah and the friend who was going to share the cottage with her discussed the financial side of things and they both agreed it would be a struggle but they would be able to afford the cottage, so it looked as if Sarah would have somewhere to stay at last. The old saying of "If something can go wrong it will go wrong", raised its ugly head once more, the team mate who was going to share the cottage, had had news of a job that she had applied for, and that there was accommodation near to where she would be working, and that she would not be taking the option of the cottage with Sarah. Back to square one again and now Sarah was getting desperate, the training sessions were becoming more frequent in the run up to the matches to be played against Australia, and the pressure of all the training and looking for somewhere to live, was starting to tell on Sarah. When Sarah would ring home in the evening after the days training at Bisham, she sounded really down in the dumps, Sheila and I were being as positive as we could, telling Sarah that something would turn up, and as luck would have it something did.

Very good friends of Sarah, Zoe and Nick Lamb, told Sarah that they had a spare room at their house in Oxfordshire and that she could stay with them for as long as she wanted, it was a little further away from Bisham than Sarah wanted, but it would be ideal until she could find somewhere closer. Sheila and I will be forever grateful to Zoe and Nick not only for coming to Sarah's aid when she needed it, but for being fully supportive at all times.

The week of the matches against Australia had come around, the first test was on Friday night at Bisham Abbey at seven o'clock, and the second test was on the Saturday, same time. I drove up to High Wycombe on the Friday, and booked into our hotel, just time for a short nap, a shower and then back out to watch the game. It was a typical November night, cold and a little misty but dry. When we arrived at the sports ground, we parked the car and headed in the direction of the floodlights which were bathing the Astroturf in artificial light, Sarah and the GB squad were doing some pre match training, she gave us a little wave on first seeing us but then got back on with the job in hand.

I was surprised to see the number of spectators who had turned up to watch the match; we actually had a little trouble getting into a good position to view the game. It's a strange feeling as a parent watching your offspring perform; the feelings are a mixture of pride and anxiety all at the same time, urging them on to do well, and just seeing Sarah walk onto the pitch in her GB kit with all the other GB players, brought a lump to my throat, and I said to myself, "go for it kid".

The game started against Australia, and I think it came as a bit of a shock to the GB players, how fast and accurate the Australians were, because Australia scored the first goal in a matter of minutes, quite understandably though we knew that the Australian side had been touring for over a month, and these were the last two games before flying back to Australia, they were not only fit, but match fit as well, where has, the GB squad had only recently started training together, and it showed. I have watched Sarah play in numerous hockey matches and I can always tell when she isn't comfortable, and this was one of those games, she wasn't playing with her usual confidence. In the first half of the game Sarah had picked the ball up on the right after a very accurate pass to her, she then ran and dribbled the ball down the wing towards the goal, passing to another GB player in front of goal to attempt a shot at goal, which was saved by the keeper, Shelia and I thought Sarah had done well, but moments later the GB coach took her off, and she was replaced with another player. It was now half time and GB were losing 3-0 to Australia, and didn't seem as if they would score. I was amazed at the amount of players in the GB squad which were rolled on and off the pitch, sometimes it seemed as if they were only on for a minute or two and they were back off again, I thought at the time, how can anyone get into a game in such a short time on the pitch, but it was all part of Danny Kerry's master plan, which over the next few months would unfold. GB lost the first test 4-0 to Australia, who in fairness were superb athletes and dynamos on the hockey pitch, but there was still one game to play, could GB secure a win next time to make it even, personally I didn't think so.

We met Sarah the following day in the Berkshire town of Marlow; she was in quite high spirits considering the previous night's performance. Over a coffee in a quaint little coffee shop Sarah told us why Danny Kerry had taken her off, Danny didn't want Sarah playing the game she usually plays, which is running with the ball, he told her just keep everything simple, no clever stuff that will come later, Sarah accepted this but I knew she would find it difficult to hold back with her attacking style of play.

We enjoyed a little lunch together in Marlow, took a walk down by the river, and watched the rowers who use this stretch of water for their Olympic training, this reminded Sarah that one of the GB players had told her, that a guy that train's the rowers was looking for someone to share a house in the village of Hurley, just a mile up the road from Bisham Abbey, and that she was going to take Sarah to meet him on Monday, Sheila said, "third time lucky", this would be an ideal place to live for Sarah throughout her time at Bisham.

Sheila and I had an early evening meal at the hotel before setting off again for Bisham Abbey for the second match against Australia. Again it was a cold misty night, and everyone was wrapped up warm to watch the game.

Sarah wasn't in the starting line up, which I always find disappointing, but after about seven minutes Sarah came on, and seemed to be playing with more confidence, in fact all the GB players were playing more confidently, and were passing the ball around well, Australia, as the previous night, were running around as if there was no tomorrow, and again scored very quickly, after a well practised move in front of the goal. GB did well to keep the score to 1-0 before half time. The evening was getting a lot colder, and the spectators were stamping their feet and thumping their hands together just to keep warm, we're a brave lot us hockey spectators.

The second half started after a short ten minute break for the players, and I think all the spectators were glad that there was only another thirty five minutes of playing time to go. Not long into the second half

Australia scored again, this time from a short corner flicking the ball high into the corner of the net. The game restarted, and I was surprised to see a GB player dispossess an Australian player of the ball, and start a run towards the Australian goal, she passed the ball wide to Sarah, who released the ball quickly into the circle, and another GB player slipped the ball past the Australian goalkeeper, the crowd were cheering like mad, this would warm them up maybe, the score now was 2-1 to Australia with enough time remaining for GB to score again and get the draw, but this was not to be, the game finished, and Australia had proven worthy winners of both test matches, but not to take anything away from the GB squad, in the second test they had performed much better, and over the next few months we would see them improve even further, the Olympics was now nine months away, and Danny Kerry's job was to get his GB women's squad at their peak just at the right time.

Sheila and I made our way back to the hotel without having a chance even to say goodnight to Sarah, but Sunday was

Sarah's day off from training so we would have the day together, before making our way back home to Wales on Monday morning. Back at our hotel we had a night cap of a few glasses of wine before retiring to bed and to try and get some heat back into our bodies, we were absolutely freezing.

Chapter 13

We awoke on Sunday morning to find a beautiful sunny crisp day, the plan for the day was, Sarah would pick us up at around 11o'clock and take us all to Henley-On-Thames where the Royal Regatta is held each year, we would have a light lunch, and a stroll along the river Thames.
We chatted about the test matches against Australia, and it seemed as if Sarah was not too bothered about the outcome of the matches, as it was just the start of a very long process which would climax at the 2008 Beijing Olympics.

Sarah suggested that we go to the cinema that afternoon to see a new film that had come out, this we did, and we all enjoyed the film, we then went back to the hotel, and had a lovely cosy meal together, with no talk of hockey allowed, because sometimes through my exuberance, I do tend to talk about Sarah's hockey, when she doesn't want to hear any more about hockey. To finish off the evening, we all went back to our room, and watched some TV, Sheila and I had a glass of wine, and Sarah was allowed a treat, a bag of Maltezers. All in all we had had a very relaxing day, Sarah had to drive back to Bisham ready for training on Monday morning, we said our goodnights, and off she went, with a reminder to text me when she arrived, to let us know she was there safe, it's a parent thing.

Monday was a mixture of excitement and tinged with sadness, Sarah was excited because after her days training she was going to look at the house, which she hoped to share, we were a little sad to leave, after a really nice weekend. We met Sarah briefly during her break from training, said our goodbyes, and started our journey back to Wales, Sarah said she would ring in the evening, and let us know how the visit to the house she was hoping to share, went.

In the evening Sarah rang to let us know how the visit went, she sounded relieved telling us that she was going to accept the offer to share the house; the guy she was going to share with was called Bret, and worked alongside the GB rowers, she also said that he was a lovely guy and very friendly, and he was even kind enough to tell Sarah that he would pay the lion's share of the rent, because he understood her situation of not having a great deal of money coming in, they agreed that Sarah would pay £300 per month, and that included all the amenities, it was still a great deal of money considering she was only having income of £427 from the Sports Lottery fund. Bret and Sarah discussed when Sarah would move in and they agreed that it would be just after Christmas as there was a GB tour coming up, a squad was to be picked to go to Argentina for two weeks in December 2007 for three test matches, and Sarah was keen to get into that squad, then in

January there would be another tour, this time to Australia for four weeks. Sarah's training with GB was going fine, and she was very pleased when she was told that she would be one of the squad on the tour of Argentina, they would fly out to Argentina the second week in December, coming back in time for Christmas, Sarah was also told in meetings with the coaching staff, that she would more than likely be involved with the GB squad up until April 2008, when there would be a further reduction in the squad, but going to Australia depended on how she performed in Argentina, and anyone who was not in the squad for Argentina, could still go to Australia.

Sarah had played in Argentina on two other occasions, once with the Welsh squad when she was playing at under 21 level, and the other time was with an earlier GB squad, Sarah had said it was always exiting playing there because the crowd were so passionate about their hockey, and the atmosphere at the games was always intense, the Argentineans certainly didn't like to lose.

The first test match against Argentina went really well with Great Britain beating those 2-1, this was a surprise win for GB, and the crowd did not like it. The second test was totally different Argentina beat GB 3-1, but it wasn't that Argentina played any better, it was just the umpires made sure they couldn't lose by giving Argentina all the right decisions, and GB all the wrong ones. The third and final test did not fare any better GB lost 4-2, they were winning 2-0 at half time, and it looked as if GB would win the series 2-1, but the Argentinean umpires had different ideas, so in total, they sent off three of the GB squad for trivial offences, ensuring an Argentina win, mind you as Sarah told me, the way the crowd were baying for blood, if GB had won, the umpires would have been lucky to get out alive.

The tour to Argentina had been a very good test of the fitness and stamina of the squad and gave the coaches some idea of the way the squad was developing, who was fitting in to the squad, and who was not.

Sarah settled down for another long flight home, at least she would now have a break for a week or two, and enjoy Christmas at home. Sarah flew into Heathrow airport, and then had to drive back home to Wales, Sarah has always resented paying the bridge toll fees to come into Wales, but is always cheered up by the sign on the side of the motorway saying "Welcome To Wales".
Driving up the A470 always pleases Sarah, the Brecon Beacons towering ahead of her, knowing that in another 15 minutes or so, she will be able to look at these beautiful mountains through her bedroom window.

Back home relaxing with a cup of hot chocolate with marshmallows floating on the top Sarah relates her trip to Argentina, how trying to run in temperatures of over 30 degrees was crippling, with the crowds booing at every move they made, but we knew that she was tough enough to take it, you have to be tough to be a top class hockey player. I asked Sarah about the forthcoming trip to Australia, she replied that they would be informed by email in the first week of January who would be going, saying that she would really love to be in that squad.

Christmas came and went, and it seemed quieter this year than it had for a number of years, with just family visiting us, and we visiting family, but for Sarah slightly different, she still had her training to do, and in total she just had one day off, Christmas day.
Sarah is lucky in one respect regarding her training, we have a sports centre just a few minutes away, and we also have an old road which used to be the main road over to Aberdare which is now closed, it is quite steep climbing up parallel to the Heads of the Valleys road, and is ideal for Sarah to do her sprinting up this hill, the fitness programme designed specifically for the GB squad is emailed to all the athletes on a regular basis with any changes incorporated. I often would say to Sarah "why don't you give the training a miss today, no one would know" maybe because the rain was bucketing down, just to see her reaction, and she would always say back "I would know, and I would only

be cheating myself, no one else". That's commitment.

Chapter 14

The first week of January 2008, I was in my computer room, which is next to Sarah's room, I could hear Sarah saying "yes, yes" she had been waiting for the email to come through regarding the squad that would fly out to Australia, and once again Sarah had been selected. The tour of Australia was planned as five matches in Perth and four matches in Brisbane; this was going to be a long tour in very hot conditions as it was summertime in Australia. A squad of twenty two players had been selected for this trip, the squad would be split into groups of players and then those players would share an apartment with each other during the tournament.

With Christmas over it was now time for Sarah to move back up to Bisham, but this time she would be staying in Hurley which is just about a mile from Sarah's training ground, with her new house mate Bret.

We packed Sarah's car full to the brim with all the stuff she would need for her new room, and Sheila and I had planned to drive up to Hurley just before Sarah was due to fly out to Australia taking with us any other things Sarah may need and also to say goodbye and good luck for the tour of Australia.

Sarah's move to Hurley was a godsend, we knew she was safe, Bret was looking out for her, and she was in close range for all the training required of her.

Sheila and I had planned to drive up to Hurley on a Friday afternoon, we were staying in a lovely bed and breakfast house which was also in Hurley, right by the river Thames, and just a five minute walk from Sarah's house, we planned to stay Friday to Sunday and come home on Monday morning, the day that Sarah would fly out to Australia.

We had a great weekend, and it was a pleasure to meet Bret, Sarah's housemate, we took him a few bottles of wine to show our appreciation for him looking after

Sarah. We had to say goodbye to Sarah on the Sunday night, as the team had to get to Heathrow quite early in the morning for their flight to Australia.

It felt strange as we made our way home seeing the huge jumbo jets coming out of Heathrow, thinking that Sarah may have been on one of them, and Sheila and I waved to them saying," take care have a great trip".

Back home once again in Wales, we knew that Sarah and the GB squad had a huge mountain to climb playing against the Australian sides, but it wasn't all about winning, the main objective was to see how they had progressed from when they had last played against Australia, and also to see how their fitness and stamina would cope with the humidity and heat of Australia.

Chapter 15

The GB team were flying British Airways to Australia, with a 5 hour stopover in Singapore. Sarah had said that she wanted to buy a new camera, as there was a problem with her old one and she didn't want to miss a month of photo opportunities in Australia, Singapore was an ideal place to buy the new camera.

The tour of Australia was being split into two parts, there was to be nine matches in total five in Perth, and then fly right across the country, where they would play four matches in Brisbane. So the first stop was Perth, the team would stay in apartments, where four of the team would each share one of these apartments. Once the accommodation was sorted and everyone settled in it was down to business, training, training, and more training.

There were three matches planned against Australian University sides, and two full tests against the Australian full senior squad, the matches against the University sides came first, and the first game which was on a Tuesday saw the GB side win 2-1, and as we were not able to contact Sarah at this time, the only way we could find out the scores, was to wait for them to be published on the GB Hockey web site. The team would then rest, with just light training, until the next game three days later; again the GB side won 2-0. Back home we were pleased that the team had won two of their three games, with just one more University side to play on the following Monday, the real tests were looming.

Monday saw the GB team draw the final match against the University side 1-1, again except for the match reports on the GB web site; we didn't know how Sarah had been performing, because this tour was crucial if Sarah was to progress further with the GB squad heading towards that goal of the Beijing Olympics being held in August.

The first full test, where Sarah would earn another GB cap was to be held in Perth on a Thursday night at 19.30 local time, and the news we received back home was not good, GB had lost 5-0, this was a disaster, but in the match report Sarah had been mentioned for playing well, this lifted our spirits, with fingers and everything else crossed for the next test.
The final test against Australia in Perth, before the GB team were to fly to

Brisbane was being held on Saturday, again at19.30 local time.
The wait for the score to come onto the GB web site was agonising, but again it was not good news they had lost 2-1, not as bad as the first test, but they had failed to get the draw which the match report said they should have had. One of the GB defence had made a crucial mistake in the dying seconds of the game, allowing the Australians to score the winner.

Chapter 16

Brisbane here we come. After packing all of their clothes and kit, the GB squad were ready for another journey, this time flying for five hours right across the country, from the west coast to the east coast.
Again the squad were to be split into groups of four and stay in apartments, with two squad members sharing a room together. The rota of who stayed with whom, was changed so that all team members mixed together not just on the playing field.

The Brisbane matches were planned out, as one match against a local University team, and three test matches against Australia, with the University match coming first.
Tuesday night again saw the GB squad with an impressive win of 5-1, but it was not the University sides they needed to beat, with three tests coming up; they needed to improve on the last games against Australia.

The night of the first test GB lost 2-0, this was not good, and they continued the run of losses with a 5-2 loss, and a 1-0 loss, but again in the match reports, Sarah seemed to be playing well, and we would know from Sarah, first hand soon, as the team were now ready to fly back home after an exhausting month of training and playing in Australia.

Unlike previous tours abroad, we would not be meeting Sarah at Heathrow and driving her back home to Wales, as now she was living in Hurley, and she would go home from Heathrow to there.

The team were arriving back at Heathrow at 6 o'clock in the morning; I had checked on Teletext that the plane had arrived safe, but Sarah also sent me a text message saying that she had arrived safely back in Hurley, and that we would speak later on that evening.

Sarah rang later that night and told us all about her trip to Australia, she was very disappointed with the losses against Australia, but Sarah was pleased with the way she had played herself. Sarah said that she had missed us and would love to see us as soon as possible, so we arranged to drive up to see her on the following Friday, we would stay Friday, Saturday and Sunday night giving all of us a chance to catch up.

This time Sheila and I stayed in Reading, travelling up and down the M4 to Hurley to visit Sarah, it was lovely once again to see her and find out how the tour to Australia had gone, we all knew there was still a very long journey ahead of Sarah before she would know if she had been selected to play for her country in an Olympics.

This trip was also different in that Sarah would not start training again until the following Wednesday, giving her a few days to readjust, and get over the jet lag, so this time we had more time to spend together even managing to get into London and going to see a West End show, we decided to go and see Chicago which we all enjoyed but if I'm to be honest, I think it was a show more suited to women. We also managed to fit in a trip to Windsor in the time we were up with Sarah, it was great not having to rush back to Bisham all the time for Sarah to do her training.

On Monday morning, we met Sarah at her house in Hurley, and decided to go for some lunch at Marlow which was just a mile or so from Hurley. Sarah had found a lovely little Bistro, which served great food; they also did an all day breakfast, which I had and it really hit the spot, great just before a long drive back home to Wales.

During our lunch, Sarah told us that the next matches that were to be played would be in Spain, again expressing her wish to be selected, I said, "yes it would be great to be selected, but they may try out some other players, and you have just come back from a great trip to Australia", Sarah agreed, but I could see by her face, that not being selected would not go down well with her. We drove Sarah back to Hurley, said our goodbyes yet again, and started our trek back home to Wales; it would be two weeks before the team selection for Spain would be announced.

Chapter 17

On the following Wednesday after our return from visiting Sarah, training started in earnest once again. Three times a day Sarah would travel from Hurley to Bisham Abbey, starting at 9 o'clock in the morning, and sometimes not finishing until 10 o'clock at night. Hockey training, weight training, meetings, and then more hockey training. Keeping up with all of this, and trying to stay injury free was taking its toll on some of the other team players, but fortunately for Sarah she seemed to be coping with it all, although she was having a few problems with her back, which she was having acupuncture for, and she was also having problems with a toe that she had broken in a game out in Rotterdam, the doctors injected the toe, saying that it should be ok for a few months, and that did seem to do the trick. On the day of selection for the tour to Spain, I received an email from Sarah saying that she had been selected and also an attachment of all the other players who had been selected and details of where they were playing, and the times of the games

The games were to be held in Terrassa, just inland from Barcelona, there were to be three matches' two training matches and one test match.
Already my brain was working overtime, would it be possible to fit a trip to Spain in. A few days in the sun would be lovely, but unfortunately, Sheila could not get the time off work, this would be the case on a number of occasions, when Sarah needed us as a family to be there with her.
The GB squad were to fly to Barcelona early on Friday morning, then play a

training match in the evening against the Spanish side.

The game started at 6 o'clock local time, and although GB played well the end result was a 0-0 draw.

The next match was a test match and caps would be awarded to the players named in the squad, and although GB were the dominant side and were winning 2-1 with only 6 minutes to go, the game again ended up as a draw 2-2, the Spanish captain scoring in the last minutes of the game. The final match was held on the Monday morning which after, the team would fly back to the UK. This was also a training match, but GB had a breakthrough, and won the game 1-0. This was a very good tour for the GB squad as Spain would be one of the teams they would meet in Beijing.

As usual Sarah sent me a text message when she arrived safely back into the UK, telling me that she would ring later in the evening and tell us more of her trip to Spain.

When Sarah did ring in the evening it was good news, she had played well, and even the coaches had commented on her performance, the long slow trail to Beijing was still being made, and with Sarah's confidence growing daily it was looking far more promising that she would come close to being selected for the Beijing Olympics 2008.

So far Sarah had been selected for all the matches that GB had played and had not missed out on any of the team selections, and as a family we were all saying, "well so far so good", but as I kept saying there was still a long way to go.

Chapter 18

Where to next? That's the question I put to Sarah when we next spoke.
Apparently the next set of matches would take place out in Ireland, in Dublin. The games were to be played against the Irish national squad at the end of March, three games in three days one on the Friday, one on Saturday, and the last one on Sunday. Sarah had again been selected, and they would fly on the Thursday from Heathrow to Dublin, all the matches were

to be played at, University College Dublin.
The GB squad were now a lot fitter, and playing a lot tighter mainly because they were starting to jell as a team, with the majority of them having played like Sarah in most of the previous tours and matches.

The first game on the Friday took place in the pouring rain, with a lot of wind blowing around the pitch making it difficult to control the ball, Sarah scored the first goal in just twelve minutes, and in the twenty eighth minute another goal was scored making it 2-0, and within another five minutes GB had scored another two goals, half time it was 4-0 to Great Britain.
In the second half GB did not dominate the game as much as they had done in the first half, but in the fiftieth minute they scored again making it 5-0, the Irish side who are by no means a weak side were taken by surprise at the strength of the GB side, and had to accept a loss of 5-0 at the end of the game.

The second game on Saturday did not start well for GB, Kate Walsh the GB captain had been taken ill, and Crista Cullen had to pull out with a broken finger from the previous day's play, so the squad had to be changed around for this game.

With quite a good crowd of spectators Ireland were cheered on and were the first to break the deadlock scoring in the seventeenth minute, 1-0 to Ireland. There was no further scoring in the first half, and Britain was playing more defensively, than in their previous match.

The second half saw GB playing more strongly, probably after a severe talking to at half time from head coach Danny Kerry, but they could still not get the ball into the Irish net, although Mel Clewlow came very close from a penalty corner, but it was well saved by the Irish keeper. It looked like Ireland was going to win this match, but in the sixty fourth minute, Alex Danson deflected the ball high into the oppositions net, it was now 1-1, the score remained at this for the rest of the game, GB would have to settle for the draw.

The final match on the Sunday morning was uninspiring for both teams for most of the first half, where neither team managed to score, with an impatient crowd of spectators urging Ireland on, but the second half saw GB playing with much more vigour and scored two goals in quick succession, 2-0 to GB. Ireland retaliated in the sixtieth minute making it 2-1 with the mainly Irish crowd of spectators going mad, but in the sixty third minute Alex Danson once again showing her talent scored what was to be the winning goal, Great Britain 3 Ireland 1.

Head coach Danny Kerry was very pleased with his team's performance and had the difficult task of ensuring that they peak at the right time, to early and they would not be at their best for Beijing, to late would find them struggling with the pressure pot of the Olympic games, the balance had to be perfect.

Another plane ride back to Heathrow on the Sunday night for the GB squad, but with two days off from training to recover from the three games played in Ireland, Sarah had a little time to herself.

Chapter 19:

At 9.0 am on the following Wednesday morning Sarah found herself once again on the hockey pitch at Bisham Abbey, the few days that Sarah had had off from training had gone quickly, Sarah and a few of the other hockey team members had managed to fit in a meal in the evening and also found time to go to the cinema, but now it was back down to business, and back to the three times a day training, starting this morning with three hours of hockey practise.

The next set of test matches were to be held at Reading Hockey club, where Great Britain would play two test matches against Argentina, again these games would show how far the GB side had progressed, because Argentina were one of the best hockey teams in the world. There was to be a twenty player team selected for these test matches, and once again Sarah was in the selection.

The first game was on a Monday evening early in May, as usual Sheila and I had travelled up to Reading and booked into a Travel Lodge to stay the few days that the games were on. After checking in we made our way to Reading Hockey club, thank goodness for satellite navigation, because some of these hockey clubs are in strange places, on arrival we were shocked to see how many spectators were there, it had been a lovely day weather wise, and the evening was warm and the sun was still shining, and the crowd of spectators were making the most of it.

At seven o'clock the game got under way, the first half saw no goals, and the sides looked pretty equal, we don't know what head coach Danny Kerry said to the girls at half time, but they started the second half with great vigour, but in the fortieth minute Argentina scored, 1-0 to the Argentineans.
Continuing to push forward the GB side managed to get a short corner, and everyone knows that a short corner gives you a chance to score, as long as the person taking the strike is on target. Mel Clewlow was taking the strike, and she hammered the ball into the net to score, the score was now 1-1, but four minutes later Argentina scored again, 2-1, the

spectators were cheering the GB side on willing them to win, there was also small jazz band playing on the side lines, playing Rule Britannia, but within minutes Argentina scored again it was now 3-1 and all looked lost, but with just five minutes left to play GB scored again making the final score 3-2, this GB side has certainly come a long way, and was showing fitness and courage and by no means were they the underdogs which they would have been a few months before, it was all starting to come together.

The following day Sheila and I travelled to Windsor to while away a few hours before the final game that evening back at Reading HC.

Windsor is a lovely place, with Windsor castle being the main attraction; we strolled down to the river Thames, and decided to take a trip on one of the many river cruises that are on offer. The scenery was beautiful and looking at the stunning million pound houses which line the river bank, making us think "how the other half live".

Bringing us back to reality was the second test that evening against the Argentineans. The match was again at seven o'clock, and once again it was warm and sunny. Carys Hopkins a brilliant forward who plays for Wales was making the journey up from Cardiff, with her parents Dave and Jane to support Sarah and the GB squad, and we were to meet them at the hockey club, we arrived first, and waited for the Hopkins family to arrive, after greeting our friends, and having a refreshing drink, we all strolled out to watch the second test match. The hockey club was even more crowded for this second test, and the jazz band had started playing early, we picked a spot about half way between both goal posts, the teams came on to the pitch and the crowds were shouting GB, GB, GB, it was a great atmosphere, Dave said to me "Sarah is looking strong and fit" all the weight training was starting to show with her biceps bulging under the GB shirt she was wearing.

The whistle blew and the second test match was under way, the GB side surged forward breaking through the Argentinean defence, were GB going to score early in the game, the answer was yes Rebeca Herbert scored the first goal making it 1-0 to GB, I think it took the Argentineans by surprise, because their heads went down, and you don't see that from these world class players very often.

Six minutes before half time Luciana Aymar one of the best players in the world struck the ball high and fast into the GB net, score at half time was 1-1, this was a great first half for the GB side. The second half started, and within ten minutes GB had scored again, 2-1 to GB, another goal from Laura Bartlett a few minutes later shook the Argentineans. It was now 3-1 to Great Britain, and once again the heads dropped on the Argentineans, but they are not a side that give up easy, and were once again on the attack, and when they do attack it is at pace and precise, and it caught the GB defence off guard, Argentina had scored, it was now 3-2 and this match could go either way, but in the sixty fourth minute Mel Clewlow once again crashed home a goal from a penalty corner, and it was goodnight Argentina final score 4-2 to Great Britain.

This had been a tremendous performance from the GB side; Sarah had not scored but had been instrumental in two of the goals scored, and her pace on the ball was stunning, with very accurate passing of the ball to her team mates.

Chapter 20

We had a quick chat to Sarah but as usual she had to zoom off for a post match meeting, but we had arranged to meet the following day before we headed back to Wales.

We said our goodbyes to the Hopkins family thanking them for making the long journey up from Cardiff to support Sarah and her GB team mates; we made our way back to the Travel Lodge for a glass of wine and a bite to eat, and a well earned night's sleep.

The following morning we drove to Sarah's house just to say goodbye, before we travelled home, she was tired, but in very good spirits, knowing that she had played well the night before.

People don't realise just how much playing two test matches in two days takes it out on your body, not just the intensity of the matches, but the physical hammering your body gets from being barged, the ball slamming into your legs, being hit with the hockey sticks, it's not a game for the feint hearted, but as I have said before, if you want to play in an Olympic games you have to have the heart and courage of a lion, only the strong will survive this sort of punishment, and Sarah had it all.

Once again Sheila and I travelled back to Wales, it had been a good trip away, the weather had been kind to us, and the hockey had been superb, and with the win against one of the world's best sides Argentina, Great Britain were now showing themselves as true contenders for an Olympic Games medal.

There were just two more tournaments to go, and just one tournament before the eighteen players would be named who would participate in the Beijing Olympic Games. The first tournament which was

again to be played out in Dublin was the Sentanta trophy. Sentanta were a company, that showed all kinds of sport on the Sky channel, and they were sponsoring this particular trophy.
As this tournament was being televised by Sentanta, I took out a subscription, so that Sheila and I could watch the matches from home.

The eighteen players who would be involved in the Olympic Games would be told by email on the Wednesday after this tournament, the date the eighteenth of June 2008, which happened to be Sheila's birthday, but first, once again Sarah had to wait to see if she had been chosen to play in the Sentanta trophy.
Sarah was obviously on edge waiting for the email to come through to tell her if she had been selected or not, I said "well, you have been picked for all the other tournaments, so perhaps Danny Kerry will give some other players a chance before final selection is made", Sarah replied "Dad, if I am not selected for this Ireland tour, I will not be going to any Olympic games", I was only trying to comfort her,

but what I had said, was not what she wanted to hear.

Sarah called us as soon as she had the email to say she had been selected for the Sentanta trophy, she was really excited about the prospect of playing in this tournament, mainly because she knew that if she played well, she would stand a very good chance for Olympic selection, and the other plus for this tournament, was that it was being televised, which is always a good thing for International players, a lot more people get to see how talented you are.

Chapter 21

The Sentanta trophy was being held at University College Dublin, the matches were scheduled for Wednesday, Thursday, a rest day on Friday, a match on Saturday with the final on the Sunday.

The countries involved were, Great Britain, Germany, South Africa and Ireland. Germany was the reigning Olympic and European champions, this was not going to be a walk in the park, and Great Britain would now have to prove that they had the qualities that were needed for an Olympic squad.

In any tournament, the team you do not want to play as an opening game, are the world champions, and that's just who Great Britain were selected to play against, Germany.
The game started with Germany showing just how strong they were, and had four penalty corners in the first12 minutes of the game. In the 17th minute GB had a great chance of scoring, but Alex Danson was robbed of the ball by a German defender. In the 25th minute Natasha Keller one of the best goal scorers in the world, squeezed the ball past GB goalkeeper Beth Story to make it 1-0, the first half finished with GB down by one goal.
The second half started and strangely, GB looked the stronger of the sides with Germany making a lot of mistakes in defence, this paid off for GB when in the 37th minute Susie Gilbert scored her first GB goal, the score was now one all. This gave GB more confidence, and they started moving the ball forward more

quickly, then disaster struck when Rachel Walker was given a yellow card and sent off, Britain were now down to ten players. Germany capitalised on this and scored again in the 44th minute, 2-1 to Germany. In the remaining time both Germany and Great Britain both had chances to score but the game ended 2-1 to Germany. Having watched this game on TV I personally thought that GB had played well, and I also thought that Sarah had played well and looked confident in her running with the ball and in her near faultless passing of the ball, the commentators on Sentanta for the hockey, managed to keep getting her name wrong, calling her Sarah Morgan, who knows where they got that from, but they did say that Sarah was the only Welsh player in the GB squad, which was great to hear.

On Thursday GB were to play South Africa, again this team was going to be tough to beat, as they were no slouches when it came to playing hockey. Sarah found herself in the starting line-up yet again, as not all the players taken to Ireland played every game, some would be in the starting line-up some would be used substitutes, and two players would not play at all. Great Britain started strongly, and in the first ten minutes had a number of chances near the South African goal mouth, the South Africans looked uncomfortable for some reason, and could not stop the constant attacking of the GB squad and in the first of GB's penalty corners Mel Clewlow struck the ball home to make the score 1-0 to GB.

GB scored again in the 28th minute, and a score of 2-0 before half time, was making GB look the stronger of the two sides, again I was watching all of the action on the TV, the commentators at least had Sarah's name right today, and were also praising the way she played, saying things like, "Sarah Thomas is just too quick on that right hand wing for these South Africans", and "that is tremendous skill from the Welsh forward". Listening to these comments back at home was just one of the things that have made all of these years of running Sarah around to hockey pitches all over the country, worthwhile. Meanwhile in the 55th minute GB only scored again making it 3-0, a score that the South Africans could not catch up with. Winning 3-0 against a quality side like South Africa now showed GB coach Danny Kerry how far his team had really progressed.

The next match in the Setanta trophy was for Great Britain to play the home side Ireland. Ireland had failed in their bid to qualify for the Olympics, but had played some tough opposition in their Olympic campaign, and was not going to be a push over.

Ireland has always had a very strong women's hockey squad, and Sarah had played against them many times whilst playing for Wales mainly in the Celtic Cup tournaments, this time she would be facing Ireland as a GB team member, and Sarah knew in advance that she would be well marked mainly because the Irish team knew how she played, and many of them had come up against her speed and skill on the ball in the past.

Although the game against Ireland was exiting and Ireland had many chances to score in the first half, they failed to get the ball into the net, and even with a tremendous crowd of Irish spectators, Ireland looked lack lustre, and were unable to contain the continuous barrage of attacks which were coming from the Great Britain squad. The final score was 3-0 to GB, and to be honest GB made it look easy, this win now meant that GB would play the champions Germany in the final and having lost to Germany once already in this tournament, there was a very big hill to climb.

Sunday the 15th of June 2008 was going to be a big day for Sarah, her team Great Britain, were in the final of the Setanta Sports Trophy, against Olympic champions Germany. This was probably the most important game so far of Sarah's career. Once again the match was being televised and I sat in anticipation waiting for the game to start. The starting line up was announced, and once again Sarah was in that all important line up. Sarah did her usual three jumps into the air as she as always done before the start of any game, and the whistle blew for play to commence.

Germany as usual were very skilled, speedy and very accurate passing the ball around, and were soon attacking the GB goal, but great defending by GB kept them at bay. Great Britain also started to attack, and it caught Germany on the back foot and for the first time we could see a chink in their armour, they soon started to get ruffled, and this gave GB a further chance to attack. Rachel Walker was working very hard on the left wing beating her opposition player with some very good ball skills, she turned the ball expertly away from the opposition and hit the ball very hard towards the circle, Sarah who had run into position caught the ball very quickly indeed and put it past the German keeper and after just seven minutes Great Britain were ahead of the Olympic champions and the icing on the cake was that Sarah had scored the goal. The TV Company showed the goal in slow motion, and even in slow motion it was amazing to see how Sarah had picked the ball up at that speed and also score the goal.

Great Britain were now having the lion's share of possession, and this was frustrating the Germans, who continued to make many mistakes, and in the thirty first minute, GB took advantage of this with Charlotte Craddock the seventeen year old forward smashing the ball high into the German goal, 2-0 to GB. Just before half time Germany were awarded two penalty corners, and I thought that they were bound to pull one goal back before half time but it wasn't the case and at half time GB were two goals ahead, this was a tremendous start to a final but there was still another thirty five minutes to go, and Germany would come out at the second half with much more determination.

The whistle blew for the second half of the Setanta Sports hockey final, GB were in the lead by two goals, but Germany would not rest on their laurels and started to attack again and were awarded a number of short corners but were unable to score mainly through the superb goal keeping of Beth Storry. In the 46th minute Alex Danson made a run into the circle, and despite falling somehow managed to reach the ball and passed it to Rachel Walker who tipped the ball into the

German goal, it was now 3-0 to Great Britain and Germany didn't seem to have the answer to stopping this onslaught by GB. The pace of the game was now frantic with Germany throwing everything they had at their GB counterparts but with no avail, and in the 58th minute Crista Cullen scored from a short corner taking the score to 4-0 to GB.

The game was now virtually over and Germany were destined to lose this final, but with just two minutes of play remaining Germany managed to pull a goal back, the final whistle blew and Great Britain were the triumphant winners of the Setanta Sports hockey final winning by 4 goals to 1.

Chapter 22:

After the Setanta final we spoke to Sarah, she was obviously delighted in winning the gold medal, and she was also pleased with her performance throughout the tournament and scoring the first goal in the final was the icing on the cake.

There was now just three days before Sarah would know if all the years of dedication to her sport of hockey would realise her dream of playing in an Olympic games.

The 18th of June 2008 was a very important day for us as a family, not only would it be Sheila's birthday, but we would finally know if Sarah had been selected to play for Great Britain in Beijing at the Olympic Games. Sarah had told us that she would be informed at 9'oclock in the morning by email, back at the Thomas household the birthday cards for Sheila's birthday were on display, the presents had been opened, the flowers that I had bought Sheila had been put in a vase by the window, but there was an air of tension throughout the house. I had bought a bottle of champagne, hopefully to toast Sarah's great news if it was to be, but also to toast Sheila's birthday, I was praying that we could toast both.

It was an agonising wait, 9 o'clock came and went, we were willing the phone to ring with hopefully good news, then at 10 past 9 the phone rang, Sheila picked the main handset up, and I picked up the extension. Sarah was crying down the phone and at first I thought she was crying through disappointment, but then I heard her say, "Dad I am going to the Olympics", once again I thumped my fist into the air as I had done so many times before, and I said to Sarah "that's fantastic news, well done, you deserve it", now we were all crying.

I quickly opened the champagne filled a glass for Sheila and myself and toasted Sarah's great news, Sarah sang Happy Birthday to Sheila, and asked her did she like the present and card that she had sent, Sheila said "you going to the Olympics is the best present I have ever had".

Sarah told us that we could not tell anyone that she had been selected until it had been made official which would be in seven days time on the 25th of June. How were we going to keep something like this to ourselves for seven days? We were on cloud nine and were desperate to share our news with someone so Sheila rang her mother, Sarah's Gran, and told her, we knew she could keep the secret, but what a secret to keep. After fourteen years of dedication to her sport, Sarah's dream had been realised.

Sheila and I thought that once Sarah had been informed of her selection, we could tell everyone, and we had told the family that we would know on the 18th of June now we had to back track, when the phone started ringing with family members wanting to know the news we had to tell a white lie, and say that due to circumstances beyond their control, GB hockey could not announce the selection, until the 25th of June, but I think the tone of our voice was giving things away, because we would have loved to have told everyone the great news.

Sheila and I made hurried arrangements to travel up to see Sarah on the weekend. We would travel up to Hurley on Friday, and come back on Sunday night. We planned to take Sarah into London so that she could choose a piece of jewellery to remind her of her great achievement. We had also planned to go and see one of the best shows in London, The Lion King.

From the beginning Sheila and I had never
even thought about travelling to Beijing to
watch Sarah in her Olympic games,
mainly due to the cost and the logistics of
travelling to China, finding somewhere to
stay and getting about Beijing once we
were there, so in my mind I had decided to
splash out more money on our trip on the
weekend to London.

On the Friday when we eventually arrived
at Hurley it was hugs and kisses and
congratulations for Sarah, to be honest it
still had not sunk in to the three of us that
Sarah was actually going to the Olympic
games.

Sarah was understandably so excited of
the prospect of playing in the biggest
sporting event in the world, and started to
tell us of what happens next. Once the
press had been officially told the names of
the hockey squad chosen to go to the
games, then we could tell all of the family,
there would be press interviews, at
Bisham and also back home in Wales.
Sarah also told us that Team GB which
she was now part of, would all have to

travel to Birmingham to be given their Team GB Beijing Olympics kit.
There was less than two months before the start of the Olympic Games in China, the opening ceremony was Friday the 8th of August 2008, Sarah would continue to live in Hurley for a few more weeks, continue training at Bisham the national sports centre, then come home before flying out to the Olympic holding camp which was to be in Macau.

On Saturday morning we picked Sarah up at her house, and then went to the train station to catch the train into London. We bought our tickets to go and see the Lion King evening performance at the Lyceum theatre.

We asked Sarah had she thought of a gift that we could buy her to remember this great moment, Sarah said she had, it was a silver necklace made by Links of London, and she also knew which store to go to, to buy it, so off we all went down Oxford street to the store where Sarah chose the exact necklace she was looking for, and to be honest it wasn't as expensive as I thought it would have been, but it was very tasteful.

We passed one store which had a mannequin in the window which was dressed in the Team GB kit so we went inside to have a closer look, a few other people came by our side who were also looking at it, and they commented on how good it looked, this was one opportunity that I wasn't going to miss and told them that they were standing next to someone who would soon be wearing it, they congratulated Sarah, Sheila and I were so proud.

It was now time for lunch; we found a lovely little Italian restaurant in Covent Garden, where we all ate Pasta and toasted Sarah with a glass of wine. After lunch Sheila and Sarah decided to go and look around the shops in Covent Garden, whilst I sat and people watched, again with a glass of wine. We still had some time to kill before the evening's performance of the Lion King, which we were all looking forward to.

After their little shopping spree Sheila and Sarah joined me, Sheila also had a glass of wine, Sarah drank water. During the conversation we were having, Sarah said, "you know Dad, most of the parents are going out to Beijing to watch the Olympic Games", I said "well we hadn't really thought about it, and it would be very expensive." Sarah said "most of the parents had had a good deal on the flight tickets, and were staying in apartments not hotels to keep the cost down." I now knew that Sarah was very keen on Sheila and I going out to Beijing to watch her play in the Olympic Games, could we do it, could we afford it.

We finished off our day at the Lyceum theatre were we watched the amazing Lion King, what a fantastic show, the music, the singing and the colours were all superb, it was money well spent, but had I know at the time that Sarah was very keen on us joining her in China I would have saved the money that I had spent on those tickets.

After the show it was time to travel back, we dropped Sarah off in Hurley, then Sheila and I made our way back to our hotel, we discussed the possibility of us travelling to Beijing, I said I would start looking into it as soon as we got back home to Wales.

Chapter 23

On Wednesday the 25th of June GB Hockey released to the press the names of the hockey squad chosen to go to Beijing, we could also now tell everyone.
Everyone was really pleased for Sarah, all saying how well she deserved it, and that they would watch every game that was on the TV.
I phoned very good friends of ours in Cardiff, Dave and Jane. Dave said it was fantastic news, and whilst I was talking to him, I mentioned that Sarah had said that she would have liked for us to go to Beijing to be with her, as we had been with her for the rest of the journey up to being chosen for the Olympics. Dave said, "if it was my daughter going to the Olympics, I would be down the bank first thing on Monday morning, borrowing the money to go", those words made my mind up for me. Sheila and I were going to finish the long journey we had all been on, by being there with Sarah in Beijing

watching her play in what Sarah had always dreamed of, playing in an Olympic games, China here we come.

Sarah had a few more weeks of training and preparation before flying out to the GB hockey holding camp in Macau on the 22nd of July 2008, the GB hockey squad would then continue to train and play friendly hockey matches in Macau, and also acclimatise to the hot and humid weather which they would encounter when they arrived in Beijing. The squad would remain in Macau for two weeks before flying out to Beijing, where the squad would then be transported to the Olympic village; this would be their home until the closing ceremony of the Olympic Games.

Mean while back home in Wales I was making enquiries with other parents that were intending to go to Beijing, mainly the GB goalie Beth Storry's parents, Malcolm and Celia, about accommodation and flights, because there was no point in booking a flight and then not being able to get accommodation, and vice versa.

Celia Storry had informed me that there was a company on the internet that was renting out apartments specifically for the Olympics, and that they had booked their flight to Beijing with Air France.

I contacted the company in Beijing, who sent me details of a number of apartments, with photos and prices. Sheila and I decided on a mid price range of apartment which was to cost £1600 for two weeks, I had to send a 20% deposit straight away to secure the apartment. This was a rather harrowing time because I was sending money to a company I didn't know, and didn't even know if when we arrived in Beijing there would be accommodation waiting for us, but all the parent who had booked through the same company were in the same boat, and it was too late now, we were committed.

We also booked our flights to China with Air France which worked out the cheapest airline at £585 per person for a return flight, and there was still a lot to do. Sheila and I both had to have a visa to enter China, and this turned out to be a real pain to get, you had to have confirmation of where in Beijing you were staying, easy if you were staying in an hotel, not easy staying in an apartment, you also had to have a copy of the passport of the person inviting you to China, again not easy because the passport holder had to be Chinese, and the guy I was dealing with named Dennis, was Dutch.

We eventually got all the documentation we needed for the visas, this was all sent off to a company of solicitors in London who specialised in getting Chinese visas, they checked all the documentation, made the appointment at the Chinese embassy, and also then went to collect the visas, which were duly sent back to us, again this did not come cheap.

Ok, so our flights are booked, our accommodation is booked, but there was still a lot of preparation to do for the trip, like finding out how close we were staying to the Olympic Hockey green, where all the hockey games were to be played. Dennis the Dutch guy who organised our apartment said that we were only about five minutes away, but looking at the maps that were available on the internet, I thought he was wrong, he kept telling me that we were only five minutes away from the Birds Nest the main Olympic dome, we would have to wait and see.

Chapter 24

Sarah in the meantime was still training and playing hockey at Bisham, the team were to go to Birmingham to collect all of their Olympic kit. Whilst they were up in Birmingham four of the GB squad were to go to the East Midlands safari park to be filmed with a new set of white lion cubs, Sarah was to be one of the four, and it was great to watch her in her new GB kit on the evening news.

The plan for Sarah now, was that she would leave the house that she had been staying at in Hurley close to Bisham, on Friday the 18th of July 2008, and come home to Wales. Sheila and I would then take Sarah up to Heathrow the following Tuesday, where Sarah would meet the rest of her team mates before flying out to the Macau holding camp, but on the Monday prior to her departure there was to be a media day for Sarah at the Welsh Institute of Sport in Cardiff, where all the Welsh TV crews and reporters would meet to interview and film Sarah before going to the Olympics.

Sarah arrived home on the Friday to a house filled with banners and balloons to celebrate her great achievement, it was great to have Sarah home again all be it for a short while. Sarah wanted to show us the Olympic kit she had received, it was amazing, whoever put all this kit together was a genius, and there was nothing that they had not thought of, even right down to a video camera for the opening and closing ceremonies.

Sarah had shirts, shorts, hats, toiletries all which had the team GB logo on; even pin badges had been made to give to family and friends.

On the Saturday night, all our family came to our house, we had a few drinks, and everyone was eager to listen to Sarah telling us of what was going to happen over the next few weeks, about the holding camp, then the journey to Beijing, and the Olympic village.

Sarah then told us the sad insight to part of the squad selection, nineteen players were selected, but only sixteen named players would stay in the Olympic village. Nineteen players would travel to the holding camp in Macau, if no one got injured, on the day that the squad flew to Beijing, one of the other three players would fly back home to the UK, the other two players would fly with the squad to Beijing, but live outside of the Olympic village in an apartment. If one of the named sixteen players was then injured during the games, one of these two would then take their place, we were grateful that Sarah was one of the named sixteen; it must have been heartbreaking for those other three players, and their parents.

The media day in Cardiff on Monday was fantastic, there were TV crews from all the regional TV stations, there were reporters from all the papers, family, friends and supporters were all there along with members of the Welsh Hockey Union.

It was strange watching Sarah in her Team GB kit being interviewed by five reporters at the same time, cameramen were taking her picture, TV crews were filming her whilst she played hockey with two young hockey players from Wales, even Sheila and I got interviewed, which neither of us really liked.

After the TV crews and reporters had finished the WHU invited all of us to a small reception at the Welsh Institute of Sport, where again Sarah was congratulated, and presented with a bouquet of flowers. Linda Treharne, Sarah's first coach with Dowlais Ladies hockey club gave a speech, and so did Margaret Medlow, Sarah's first Welsh coach, I had a lump in my throat listening to Margaret, saying that from the first time she had seen Sarah play she knew that Sarah had a special talent and would go far, but to be selected to go to an Olympic games, and be only the third Welsh player to be selected and the first outfield player ever was amazing.

Sarah had one more night at home before the start of her journey of her dreams, the Olympic Games.

Tuesday morning, Sheila, Sarah and I set off for Heathrow Airport terminal 5; Sarah was to meet the rest of the squad, and all the other people involved and needed to compete in an Olympic games, at two o'clock inside the terminal.

Sarah was dressed in the Team GB travelling track suit, which looked absolutely superb, the car was full of everything she needed for over a month away in Macau and China.

Prior to leaving for China, the team manager contacted me and asked, without Sarah knowing, if we could send him a good luck, congratulations card, these would be placed on the pillow of the team players beds in their rooms in the Olympic village when they arrived, I thought it was a lovely touch.

After a few hours driving we arrived at the brand new Heathrow terminal 5, it's a fantastic terminal, and you can actually stay for a few minutes to drop off passengers.

There was a porter standing by, keeping an eye out for people who overstay their drop off time, we took Sarah's luggage from the boot, we said our goodbyes, gave Sarah huge hugs and kisses, and told her to enjoy every moment of this wonderful experience.

Sarah didn't have her Team GB tracksuit top on at this time, so I told her to put it on, when she put it on, the porters eyes turned towards her, and he then knew that Sarah was not just an ordinary passenger, she was an elite athlete going to the Olympics, he gave her a huge smile and said good luck as she passed.

From the whole of Wales there were only eleven athletes chosen to go to the Beijing Olympics, and our daughter was one of them, it can't get better than that, we were such proud parents.

Sheila and I made our way once again back to Wales, knowing that in a few weeks time, we would be joining Sarah in China, living the dream with her.

One of Sarah's sponsors had asked Sarah to write a blog on their website of her experiences both in Macau and in Beijing, Sarah had taken her laptop with her, so that she could also stay in touch with us, Sarah would email every day after training and playing in Macau, letting us know of what it was like, she did say the heat and humidity were very oppressive, and it was very difficult to play in those conditions. Sarah told us how lovely Macau was, and that it was full of casinos, because the Chinese were gambling mad. Sarah also told us that the team were slightly on edge when training and playing, not wanting to get injured, and being sent back home to the UK, the team were also very keen to get to Beijing and the start of the Olympics proper.

The GB hockey squad were to stay in Macau, training and acclimatising for two weeks, before flying to Beijing.
They were to leave on the 5th of August for Beijing, the Olympic opening ceremony was on the 8th of August 2008, and the whole world was waiting in anticipation to see what the Chinese had in store for that opening ceremony, the Chinese had spent 20 billion dollars on

their preparation for holding the Olympics, some people had said it should have never been held there, not just because of their politics, but there was great concern for the amount of air pollution in Beijing, and would it affect the athletes, the world would have to wait and see.

Chapter 25

The day had come for the GB hockey squad to leave their holding camp in Macau, prior to the Olympics, for Beijing. Security in Beijing was extremely high due to threats from certain factors in China, threatening to disrupt the Olympic Games, and threats on athlete's lives. Sarah told us that when they arrived at Beijing airport they were ushered through to a secure area, and then taken to their coach surrounded by armed police, the roads had been closed off and they were escorted to the Olympic village, with police cars both in front and behind the coach, Sarah said it was very intimidating, but the excitement of actually seeing the

Olympic village for the first time was
overwhelming.

Arriving at the Olympic village all the GB
hockey team were given security
clearance, and security tags which had to
be worn at all times, and no one was
allowed out of the village at all, this was
to be their cocoon until the end of the
Games.
The team were shown to their rooms,
which had all been decorated in their
personal photos, an Olympic Teddy Bear
was placed on each bed, and on each
pillow was the good luck card sent from
each player's parents.
The Chinese Olympic helpers of which
there were literally thousands, were on
hand to help the athletes with anything
they needed, if the athletes needed any
laundry doing or assistance in any way
these helpers, were on hand twenty four
hours a day.
Sarah said the Olympic village food hall
was amazing, she said when she first
walked in and saw famous athletes from
all over the world and from all different
sports, famous tennis players, famous

basketball players, all sitting and eating together, and it was surreal.

Back home in Wales each night the regional TV companies would highlight one of the Welsh athletes who were in Beijing, and Sheila and I waited patiently for Sarah's night to be highlighted, and it was fantastic, she spoke so well and with such confidence, she commented on how much she would love to come home with an Olympic medal, but she was also aware of the very tough opposition that she would be playing against, and that people had to remember that the GB squad were ranked eleventh out of twelve in the world, and it was not going to be easy, especially playing in that heat and high humidity.

Sheila and I were now all prepared for our journey to China, we were to take the coach from Cardiff up to Heathrow airport on Saturday morning, the 9th of August, the day after the opening ceremony, we were then going to fly to Charles De Gaul airport in France, before getting our connection flight from France to Beijing.

The total flight time was to be around twelve hours, I did not particularly like flying, and the furthest I had flown before was to Spain on holiday, Sheila just took it all in her stride.

At two o'clock local time and eight o'clock Beijing time on Friday the 8th of August 2008, the opening ceremony of the Beijing Olympics began, and from the first opening scenes, we knew that this ceremony was going to be something special, and it was, we were in awe, at how much work and detail the Chinese had put into their opening ceremony, it said to the world, we know we have failed in the past, but we are trying to put the future right.
There was a different theme for different ages in the Chinese existence, and each and every one, was more impressive than the last, the ceremony started to culminate with the appearance of all the athletes from all the countries taking part in the Games.
Sheila and I waited patiently for the arrival of Team GB, and to see Sarah in her opening ceremony outfit, we had seen

it previously when she had brought all her kit home, but had not seen her dressed up in it. Then the cameras went back stage, and we could see Team GB just putting their jackets on, ready for their first walk out into the very impressive Birds Nest arena.

There were eighty thousand people in the Birds Nest that night, including the American president, George Bush.

The heat and humidity in there must have been appalling, and when the cameras went again backstage, we caught our first glimpse of Sarah, dressed in her Olympic opening ceremony outfit, and she looked fantastic, her face was beaming, and glistening with the heat.

The moment finally came and Team GB came out to thousands of people cheering them, they all walked behind Mark Foster who had been giving the honour of carrying and waving the Union Jack flag, Sheila and I were glued to the TV trying to catch a glimpse of Sarah, and then, there she was waving her little Union Jack flag for all she was worth, this is what all those hours, months and years of training, dedication and determination were for. Sarah was finally at the destination, that she had set her sights on many years before. Sheila and I, both had tears in our eyes, but they were tears of joy.

The Olympic torch high above the Birds Nest was lit in the most spectacular fashion, the Games had begun.

Chapter 26:

On Saturday morning, before the start of our journey to Beijing, I was both excited and apprehensive. I was to drive our car to our friends, Dave and Jane Hopkins on the outskirts of Cardiff, we were going to leave our car with them whilst we were away and they would then take us to the coach station, and pick us back up on our arrival home.

It was a strange feeling leaving Merthyr Tydfil, knowing that the following day we would be half way across the world in China.

The coach journey up to Heathrow airport was quite pleasant; it was lovely to let someone else do the driving for a change. Our flight to Charles de Gaul airport in France was from terminal 3 at Heathrow, we carried our luggage to an Air France check in desk, and we were quickly and efficiently checked in, we would not see our luggage now until we reached Beijing.

Sheila and I made our way to one of the many bars in the terminal, and we ordered a bottle of wine as we had over two hours to wait for our flight to France. Sheila loves just to sit and people watch, and I wondered what different parts of the world all these people would end up in.

Eventually our flight number to France was called, there had been a delay in the incoming plane, and we were now cutting it fine to get to France and make our connection to Beijing.
On the flight to France I kept looking at my watch, as our connection was due to leave from Charles De Gaul to China at seven o'clock in the evening, by the time we landed and disembarked from the

plane we would only have about twenty minutes to get to our connection departure lounge.

About twenty minutes before we were due to land, a stewardess came to Sheila and I, and asked us to move to seats which were nearer the exit, so that we would have more time to get to our connection flight, this was a good idea, as it did give us a few more minutes to get to the departure terminal.

As soon as the planes doors were open the stewardess let Sheila and I off, and then it was a mad dash to get to our connection departure lounge, once we arrived there we were again rushed through to the waiting aircraft by airport staff, we had made it with just minutes to spare.

The flight to Beijing was to be about eleven hours, but with the time difference we were due to land at ten o'clock the following morning, this was on the tenth of August 2008, and Sarah's first game of the Olympics was against Germany at nine o'clock that same night.

The flight to Beijing was uneventful, it was difficult to sleep and being sat in economy class, there was not a great deal of room; it was just a matter of trying to get in a comfortable position and trying to doze for a while. I spent most of my time looking at the flight progress screen, which also told you how many miles you had flown, how many miles to go and what time you were expected to land. I was still apprehensive about whether the guy we had paid to find our apartments would be there when we landed, and what would the accommodation be like, as we had only seen a few photos, and would we be close enough to the Olympic Green where the hockey games were being played, all of this was going through my mind.

We landed in Beijing on time, after we had disembarked; Sheila and I made our way to the luggage carousel to collect our luggage. I had been waiting about ten minutes watching all the cases go by, looking out for our cases, when Sheila tapped me on the shoulder, she pointed to a notice board, which had our names on, and saying that we had to go to a certain office.

We made our way there. There were a number of people already waiting, and these people had also been passengers on our flight. Apparently all the passengers who had travelled from London to France for the connection to Beijing were minus their luggage, great, we were in Beijing, and our luggage was still in France.

We had to fill out a load of forms which was, not easy, because of the language barrier. It was very difficult to understand the Chinese staff, which was, if they spoke English at all. Anyway we would not have our luggage for at least two days, and that it would be sent to our apartment.

It was now time to leave the terminal, and find Dennis, our man to take us to our apartments; Malcolm and Celia Storry were with us, as they were also to meet the same guy.

When we went outside the heat and humidity hit us like a thunderbolt, but the good news was, was that Dennis, our man in Beijing was standing there, holding a card, with our names on.

He was a Dutch guy but like all the Dutch, spoke good English, he commandeered two taxis, to take us to out apartments, Sheila and I in one taxi, and Malcolm and Celia in the other, at least now we knew we had somewhere to stay.

The taxi journey took about twenty five minutes; we could only use certain lanes on the road as some of the lanes were for Olympic traffic only.

We arrived at our apartment complex and it looked ok from outside, we were taken to the fifth floor where our apartment was located, we went inside and to be honest I was quite taken aback, it wasn't the best apartment in the world, and for £1600 it was extremely basic, the main room just had two beds and a TV in it, the kitchen was the smallest I had ever seen in my life, and because of its unhygienic look was never going to be used, the bathroom was just as small and just as grubby.

I thought to myself, well we are here now, we just have to make the most of it, I paid the Dennis the remainder of the money, and then he was gone, saying that he would call the following day with his partner who was Chinese so that she could talk to the people at the airport regarding our lost luggage.

Malcolm and Celia Storry were then taken to their apartment, which they told us later was slightly worse than ours, their bathroom and toilet was actually in the same room as their beds, just hidden from view with a plastic curtain, this gave me some comfort.

The first thing Sheila and I had to do was to go out and find somewhere, where we could buy some clothes to tide us over until our luggage turned up.

We left the apartment and walked to where we could see some stores, the heat and humidity was horrendous, and having been in the clothes we were in for nearly twenty four hours, were desperate for a shower and change of clothing.

A supermarket at the end of the street had everything we needed, but communicating exactly what we wanted was impossible, so we just picked up the clothes we wanted and walked to the cash desk with the Chinese assistant not leaving our side until we had paid.

It was really strange everyone was staring at Sheila and I, all these Chinese people, and two strange Europeans walking around.

We made our way back to the apartment; it seemed the area we were staying in had everything we would need for our two week stay.

Back at the apartment, Sheila commented how calm I had been over our lost luggage, I explained that there was nothing we could do, and we were stuck here, we just had to make the most of it. After a shower and change of clothes, things didn't seem so bad, whatever China was to throw at us we would deal with it, and I was not going to be disappointed.

Chapter 27

All the parents who had travelled to Beijing were to be given free tickets for all the hockey matches that were being played in Beijing. We were to pick the tickets up at a place called the GB Lodge, where Team GB had set up a club for Team GB athletes, parents and friends.

Now this lodge was situated in a part of Beijing a few miles away from our apartment, I had found it on a map, but didn't have a clue how to get there; we couldn't take a taxi, because we couldn't communicate with the driver to tell him where to take us.

Prior to leaving for Beijing, I had printed out in the Chinese language certain places that I knew we would need to get to, for example, the Olympic Hockey Green, and the Olympic Village, but I didn't have the address of the lodge in Chinese, so there was only one thing for it, and that was to walk.

Sheila and I came out of our apartment and turned right, the opposite direction from the shops and restaurants that we had been to earlier, we walked up the road for about two minutes, and were astonished to see about five minutes walk away, was the amazing Birds Nest stadium. We had only seen it on the TV and it looked fantastic, but now in view from where we were standing it was awe inspiring. With the Olympic flame burning brightly above it.

I knew that to get to the lodge we had to walk towards the Birds Nest, follow the road around, and then we would be in the area where the lodge was located; we just had to find it.

We were still being stared at by all the Chinese people that were also walking towards the Birds Nest, and I mean there were hundreds of them, it was weird.

The nearer that we got to the Birds Nest the bigger it became and the number of Chinese people increased also. As we crossed a road a Chinese girl came on to me, said something in Chinese which obviously I couldn't understand, but she made a gesture with her camera, she was with four or five other Chinese people, and I thought that she wanted me to take their picture, with the Birds Nest in the background.

I followed the girl to the rest of the party, but instead of giving me the camera to take their photo, she put me in line with the rest of her group, and started to take photos of us, that's how strange it was for them to see a European walking around, this photo taking happened a number of times and in different places.

After a walk that I wouldn't want to do again, we eventually found the lodge. From the outside it was very inconspicuous, with Chinese guards on the outside, they opened the gate for us, and we entered a lovely little courtyard. We had to sign the entrance book, then we were taken inside, where we had to have our photos taken for our security tags, which we had to wear at all times whilst in the lodge, this again was for all the athletes security.

The only way to explain the lodge was that it was a little part of Britain in China. It was decorated with all Olympic paraphernalia, there were wide screen TV's everywhere showing the events live, there was coffee and tea making facilities, and vending machines for cold drinks and water, and what's more it was all free.

The other idea with the lodge is that this is where we would meet up with Sarah during the Olympic Games; the athletes were not allowed to leave the Olympic village except to come to the lodge.

The athletes would be told a certain time that they would be leaving for the lodge,

and they would be brought there by coach, they would then have an hour or so to meet with their parents or friends and then they would be driven back again, so on a day that Sarah did not have an hockey game to play, she would text me a time, and we would then meet her there.
Sheila and I had a well deserved cold drink with Malcolm and Celia Storry, who had also turned up at the lodge, we also exchanged mobile phone numbers so that we could stay in touch whilst in Beijing, apparently their apartment, was just a ten minute walk away from ours, so we were going to arrange a few nights out together. We said goodbye to all the hockey parents who were at the lodge telling them that we would see them later, at the first game for GB against Germany later that night.

When we booked into our apartment, I had Dennis the Dutch guy, to give us the address of the apartment, in Chinese, so that we would be able to find our way back in a taxi.
It wasn't proving very successful, because as we stopped taxis on the road outside the lodge, they looked at the address in

Chinese and just shook their heads, and basically told us to get out of the taxi, we weren't aware at the time, that the Chinese government had brought in hundreds of taxi drivers from outside of Beijing, to cope with the extra demand of the Olympics.

After about five attempts at trying to get a taxi, we eventually picked a taxi driver who knew where to take us, and thankfully we made it back to our apartment, we now also had the proper address of the lodge so that we could just get a taxi to it rather than walking, which to be honest I didn't think I could do again.

Sheila and I now had time to get a few hours sleep before getting ready to go to the nights hockey match at the Olympic Green.

The game against Germany was to start at nine o'clock local time, so I said to Sheila we should leave about seven o'clock, giving us ample time to get to the hockey stadium, because up to now we still did not know where it was, or long it would take to get there.

When we came out of the apartment it was still very hot and humid, and in the distance I could hear a rumble of thunder. The apartment block was very secure with an electronic gate which you could only access with your key card, this was the entrance we had used on arrival, and the other entrance was manned by Chinese guards who saluted Sheila and me as we passed. There was a main road just outside the gates, and I said to Sheila that it looked like a good place to get a taxi, wrong again.

We stopped taxi after taxi, again showing them the address for the Olympic Hockey Green written in Chinese, they either didn't understand it, or didn't know where the hockey green was.

As we were showing yet another taxi driver the address two Chinese women came on to the scene, probably to try and help, they also looked at the address then spoke to the driver, and within minutes they were all arguing with each other, the taxi driver drove off, and that left us with the Chinese women who were now trying to explain to Sheila and I how to get to the stadium in Chinese, this was not going well, and time was moving on, the women pointed to the end of the street, and again pointed to the right at the end of the street, as if to say it is just up there.

I looked at the map that I had, and the stadium did look as if it was in that direction, I said to Sheila it looks like we will have to walk it. We headed off in the direction that the two women had shown us, by the time we got to the end of the street it started to rain, just a little drizzle at first, but it was becoming more persistent.

Sheila and I walked about a mile up the road, and the map showed that we were to turn left at the end of it, but when we got there the road had been blocked off and there were Chinese guards stopping people and traffic going in that direction. We tried a few different turnings but each time it was the same, we could not get through.

It was now raining quite heavily, we were totally lost, and the hockey match would soon be starting, it looked like we would not see Sarah play in her first Olympic hockey match.

We started to walk back the way we had come, keeping a look out for a taxi that we could flag down, but none came our way. We came upon another road turning right, but again it was not possible to use it, and the guards would not let us through, but out of the manned gates came a number of the Olympic Chinese helpers, I said to Sheila, I will ask these, to see if they could tell us how to get to the stadium. The Olympic helpers had been trained in basic English and one or two of them could just about understand us, and in fairness to them they were being helpful. The first thing they did was to provide Sheila and me with full length plastic coats to keep the rain off. They then explained that they would try and ring for a taxi to take us there, but after about twenty minutes of this there was still no sign of a taxi. We were just about to give up when a police van came down the road, the helpers flagged the police van down, and we watched as they explained to the police about our predicament.
One of the helpers waved to us to go towards the police van, the helper explained that the police van would take

us there, we thanked the helpers for all of their assistance and for the plastic coats, and Sheila and I got into the back of the police van, there were two police officers in the front of the van, and we sat in the back with another two officers.

The police officer driving the van spoke pretty good English, we showed him the ticket for the hockey stadium, and off the van went, now I thought our troubles were over, but believe it or not, the police didn't even know how to get to the hockey stadium, they were having the same problem as us, all the roads were blocked off, this was all to do with the extreme tight security that was in place to protect the athletes and the progress of the Games. Eventually I could see the floodlights over the hockey stadium, and I knew we were now close to it. The police van pulled in, and said that was as far as they could go, Sheila and I thanked them and told them how grateful we were, whether they understood or not I don't know. At least now we were in the right place, it was just a few minutes' walk to the entrance to the hockey stadium.

Chapter 28

The entrance to the Olympic Hockey Green was amazing, there was the usual team of helpers, and the security was very high, the entrance was just like an airport check in.
First your tickets were checked, then you had to walk through a scanner, if that beeped you were then subjected to a body search, all our bags were checked, you were only allowed the flag of your nation, in our case the Union Jack, the Welsh Dragon flag of Wales, which we also had was taken off us, I was really annoyed by that, but those were the rules.

The rain was now coming down hard, and we had another ten minute walk to the actual hockey pitch, the flagstones which had been laid on the path to the pitch had not been laid very well and there were puddles everywhere, I gave up trying to keep my shoes dry, I did not have socks on, they were still in my case in France, so I could feel my feet squelching in the wet shoes.

We were very grateful though for the plastic coats the Chinese helpers had given us, at least they would stop our upper bodies getting even more wet. Sheila and I walked up the steps of the hockey stadium to find our seats. Now I had seen pictures of this hockey stadium on the internet prior to coming to Beijing, but the photos didn't give it justice, it was superb. There was seating for eleven thousand people, two huge TV screens, and the pitch itself looked flawless. This wasn't the start to the Olympic Games that I had envisaged for Sarah, pouring with rain, the wind was quite high and the sky looked really ominous.

My mind was already thinking about after the game how were we going to get back to our apartment, at that moment Malcolm and Celia Storry arrived, it was good to have some company, because they would need to get back to their apartment also.

The German squad came onto the pitch for their pre-game warm up, then Great Britain came onto the pitch, Sheila and I were looking out for Sarah, it was difficult to spot her with the rain blowing around as it was, but Sheila then said, "there she is".

We both stood up and started waving the flag around I suppose just to try and tell her that we were there, we could see Sarah looking up into the stand, and she raised her hockey stick in acknowledgement, that she had seen us.

Although Great Britain had beaten Germany out in Ireland 4-1 recently in the Sentanta Trophy final, we knew that this was not going to be easy, and the weather was not going to help at all, it was going to be difficult passing the ball around with this high wind, and the rain was still hammering down, but in fairness, both sides had to put up with it.

Both teams lined up for their countries national anthem, a camera crew were right in front of them, showing each players face on the massive TV screens around the ground, we waited patiently for Sarah's face to appear on the screen, and I must be honest she did look anxious. This was a huge moment for Sarah, after all those years of playing hockey and training, the time had come to see if she was really up to it.

The teams came on to the pitch for the start of the game, I was very disappointed that Danny Kerry had not chosen Sarah to be in the starting line up, and I knew that Sarah would not have been pleased also. During the game all sixteen players would be used, eleven would start, and then they would roll off and on between every six to ten minutes, depending on the intensity of the game.
We could see that both sides were struggling to control the ball in the dreadful weather conditions, Great Britain suddenly attacked the German goal, and a shot was taken but it went wide of the post, within minutes GB attacked again, the ball was struck across the goal from the right hand side, but the forward failed to connect with ball, and a chance of an early goal had been thrown away.

Sheila and I could see Sarah on the sideline waiting to come on to the pitch; she was waving the number of the player who was to go off in the air, and then Sarah was on the Olympic Hockey Green, Sarah's Olympics had started.

Germany scored first in the twenty sixth minute; Fanny Rinne drag flicked the ball high into the net from a penalty corner, and there was little that GB goal keeper Beth Storry could do.
 Britain continued to attack, and three minutes later Crista Cullan scored from a penalty corner, the score was now level 1-1.
Both teams looked to be on a level par, but two minutes later a lack of concentration in Britain's defence saw Germany score again making it 2-1 to Germany at half time.
The teams went off the pitch soaked to the skin, the rain had been relentless, and they now had a chance to change into dry kit for the second half.
Sarah had seemed to hold her own in the first half and had passed the ball around well, but like all the players on the pitch was struggling with the weather conditions which I must admit were

appalling, and at one point, I thought the game may be abandoned.

The second half of the match began and both Sheila and I were praying that Great Britain could find the strength and courage to come back and beat Germany, but another mistake and a poor shot at goal from one of GB's forwards, kept the game at 2-1 to Germany.

Germany on the other hand worked another penalty corner, and scored again making it 3-1, it was now going to be difficult for GB to come back from this. Fanny Rinne made it 4-1 in the fifty second minute, Germany then scored again putting the final nail in the coffin making it a 5-1 win over Great Britain.

In my humble opinion, I didn't think that Great Britain had played as well as they could have, there were some players on that pitch, who didn't put in the effort that should have been afforded to an Olympic hockey match. It's always easy to criticize from the stands as a spectator, but you can still see if a player is not putting the effort in that they should be putting in. Just that little extra push to get a ball that they failed to get might have made the difference from losing to winning. This lack of effort from certain players, the names I won't mention, but they will know who they are, carried on throughout the tournament.

Our first day in Beijing, had not been a good one, our luggage had not arrived in China, we had got lost trying to find the hockey stadium, we were soaking wet from the continuous rain, and Great Britain had lost their opening match to Germany. I didn't think it could get much worse, but I was to be proved wrong again.

Sheila and I, Malcolm and Celia, stayed for a while so that we could have a quick word with our daughters whilst they were cooling down on the pitch.

Sarah was devastated to have lost their opening match, whilst some of the other players looked as if they couldn't care less, I found this so annoying, I told Sarah to pick herself up, ready for the next match which was to be against Argentina, she said she would be fine, and I think we cheered her up by telling her we had arrived at the stadium, in a police van.

Monday was a rest day for Sarah her next game was on Tuesday against Argentina at eight thirty in the morning, we said goodbye to her, and told her that we would see her then.

The four of us then left the stadium; we now had to find a taxi each to take us back to our apartments. We walked for about fifteen minutes before we found a spot where taxis seemed to be picking up and dropping people off. Two taxis arrived together, we said goodbye to Malcolm and Celia, telling them that we would contact them the following day.
It was now eleven thirty at night; Sheila and I were very tired, very wet, and just wanted to get back to our apartment.
I showed the taxi driver our address in Chinese and off he went, I thought good at least he knows where to go, wrong again, he didn't have a clue.
We were driving around for an hour and a half with him trying to find the address. He would pull up one street, then stop, then turn around and go back the way he came, he even stopped at a late night shop to ask directions, but all to no avail. It

came to the point where I thought we may be in the taxi all night, then all of a sudden, Sheila said, "that's the supermarket, where we bought our clothes today" I indicated to the driver to turn right at the next junction, and lo and behold, we were in the street of our apartment, were we glad to get out of that taxi.

The apartment we had was not the best in the world, but was I glad to get into that bed that night, we were both exhausted. My last thought before I dropped off to sleep was, did we do the right thing by coming to Beijing and the Olympics, at that moment, I believed not.

Chapter 29

As the old song goes, what a difference a day makes. We woke up to find the sun shining, and not a cloud in the sky, and there was no sign of the dreadful smog that we had all been warned about.

Sheila and I had the day to ourselves to acclimatise to our surroundings, and to discover what delights Beijing had to offer.

The next moment the apartment phone rang, I answered it, to find it was Dennis the Dutch guy as we were now calling him.

He asked me to press the button to open the door downstairs, so that he and his Chinese partner could come up. We dressed quickly and allowed them in. We explained to Dennis the problem that we had getting to the hockey the previous night, and also telling him that I had specifically asked to be as close to the hockey as possible. He said but you are, the Birds Nest is just there, as he pointed out of the window to the part of the Bird Nest we could see from our apartment. I tried to explain to him that the hockey was not being held there it was at the Olympic Green. Either he didn't understand or didn't want to understand, but I wasn't getting through to him. His Chinese partner was named Maria, she was very pleasant, and very understanding, and also far more patient than Dennis.

Maria took the phone numbers we had been given by the airport staff, saying that she would ring them and sort out the delivery of our luggage when it arrived from France; she also gave me her mobile number so that we could contact her at anytime if we needed help, or had any problems.

Dennis then suggested that we all go outside, so that he could show us where the hockey was being played, I knew it was going to be a waste of time, but we all went outside anyway. Once again the heat and humidity hit you as soon as you walked onto the street, and I wasn't in the mood to listen to any more of Dennis's nonsense.
The four of us walked to the end of the road, and once again Dennis pointed to the Birds Nest, and said there you are, just five minutes away, I again tried to explain that that was not where the hockey was being played. I pulled out my maps, and showed him; finally I had got through to him. Dennis then said that the Olympic Green was not that far away, but because all the roads had been closed off for security, it was now difficult for the taxis to get there, and most of the drivers

refused to go there. Maria suggested using the bus, I asked where the bus went from, and she pointed straight ahead, I couldn't believe it, our apartment was just two or three minutes away from the bus station.

All Sheila and I had to do now was to find out how to use the bus service that ran specifically for the Olympic Games. Dennis and Maria left saying that they would get in touch as soon as our luggage arrived, Sheila and I went back to our apartment, once we had showered and changed into pretty much the same clothes that we had on the day before, we went back out to explore our surroundings.

The first place we found was a Starbucks coffee shop, not something I would have expected to find in China, we decided to try their coffee, and also a pastry, both were very good, and the service and politeness of the Chinese waitress was great.
We were still being stared at wherever we went, but all the Chinese were pleasant and helpful, and if they could speak a little English, they were very keen to try it out.

The area of Beijing that we were staying in was very busy, the traffic seemed to be coming from everywhere, and no cars stopped at a crossing even if the lights were on red, the only time they stopped was when a Chinese local walked out in front of them, it was frightening, but we soon got the hang of it.

There was a lovely hotel in our area call the Marco Polo, and I noticed that a lot of taxis were stopping there, I said to Sheila, if I get a business card for the hotel, we can show that to the taxi drivers, when we want to get back from the lodge, it was a great idea and it worked, we never had any problems getting back after that, and the hotel was just a ten minute walk from our apartment.

There were plenty of restaurants in the area, mostly serving Chinese or Thai food, but there were also loads of Macdonalds, and KFC fast food outlets.
The outlook wasn't looking so bleak now, if we could just sort out the transport back and forth to the hockey pitch all would be fine. Another good bit of news came

through to us, our luggage had arrived in Beijing, and would be delivered to our apartment by 4 0'clock that afternoon. It was fantastic being reunited with our clothes.

During the day Celia Storry contacted me, and she explained the Olympic bus service to me, all we had to do was go to the bus station, get the number two bus, on entering the bus, you had to show your entrance ticket to whatever sport you were going to watch, and the journey was then free. Celia said to stay on the bus until it reached the next bus station, then we had to get off, and then catch the number one bus, and stay on this until it reached the next bus station, this bus station was for the Olympic Green. The busses just went around in a very big circle, they ran all day and most of the night.

Sheila and I would see how easy it really was the following day, when we had to get to the Olympic Green by eight in the morning for the eight thirty start to Sarah's next Olympic hockey match against Argentina.

Chapter 30

It was seven o'clock on the Tuesday
morning, it was already very hot in
Beijing, and Sheila and I were standing in
the queue waiting for the first bus to come
in that we hoped would get us to the
Olympic Green.
The bus came in and we got on showing
the driver our hockey match ticket, he
ignored it completely, so we just sat
down. The bus was full to the rafters, as
we started our journey; I was watching the
stops that the bus picked people up at.
At the second stop Malcolm and Celia got
on, I managed to attract their attention,
asking if they were both well.
After about twenty minutes, the bus pulled
in to the next station, and I knew that this
is where we changed busses, everyone got
off, we waited for Malcolm and Celia,
Celia knew where the next bus would be
waiting, the number one bus was already
in, so we just boarded, and off we went
again. I was starting to recognise certain
places, and I knew that the lodge was
quite near the bus station too.

After another twenty minutes or so, we arrived at the Olympic Green, the terminal where the driver dropped us off, would be where we caught the bus back to the station near our apartment, finding our way around on the bus had taken a great weight off my mind, and I will be forever grateful to Celia Storry, for sorting the transport situation out.

We made our way through security again, we only had the Union Jack flag this time, so we thought that we would go straight through, but this time for some reason, the security didn't like the snack biscuits that Sheila had brought with her, and they confiscated them, perhaps they thought we would use them as missiles to throw at the pitch, I don't know.

The four of us made our way to our seats, we then found that we would not be sitting together, but at least it was in the same row, and we were with all the other British parents.

The stadium was filling up very quickly, but we noticed that in the one stand all the spectators were dressed in the same T shirts, the Chinese government were bussing in hundreds of soldiers made to look like spectators, just to fill the venue, I suppose it looked better when the TV pictures were shown around the world.

The atmosphere was totally different to the last time we were in the stadium, the helpers were handing out different plastic toys to everyone, which made a noise when they were banged together, and the noise in the stadium was deafening, but exciting, I said to Sheila "this is more like it".

Both teams again came on to the pitch for their pre-match warm up, Great Britain were playing in their red team kit today, and they looked superb. Sarah raised her stick again to us, but whether she could see us or not in this massive crowd of spectators I didn't know.
I had butterfly's in my stomach waiting for the game to start, praying that they would play better than in the previous game , where they lost 5-1 to Germany. Conditions today were one hundred percent better though than on Sunday night, so that would help. The umpires

blew their whistles to let the teams know there was just two minutes before the national anthems.

Great Britain and Argentina lined up for the anthems, this is always a proud moment for the players and spectators alike, and everyone respects another countries national anthem, we all stood as Argentina's national anthem was played first, then it was Great Britain's national anthem, once again the TV crew held the camera on each GB players face relaying the picture to the TV screens in the stadium, today again, Sarah looked tense, there was a strain on her face that I had not seen before, I just hoped that she would have a good game.

This time Sarah was in the starting line up, I knew that she would be pleased with this; she did her usual three jumps into the air before the whistle went for the start of the match, and then the game was under way.

Argentina were on the attack, the speed and agility of this side had to be seen to be believed, although now, there were a number of the Argentinean side on the wrong side of thirty, and there was no way that they could keep this pace up for the full seventy minutes. The Great Britain defence were taken aback by the onslaught of the Argentineans and in the tenth minute Soledad Garcia a veteran of the 2000 and 2004 Olympics scored, 1-0 to the Argentineans.

As soon as the Argentineans scored you could see the heads of the GB side drop, the GB supporters shouted as one "heads up girls", "you can do this", as the game restarted GB went forward trying to break through the Argentinean defence but without much success but in 17th minute GB finally got a penalty corner, but they failed to capitulate on it, again in the 18th minute they again failed to put the ball into the net after another penalty corner, and in hockey its chances like this you have to take full advantage of.
The game continued with the Argentineans putting on the most pressure, but in the intense heat I could see that their pace was slowing slightly

but that did not stop them from scoring again just before half time, the score at half time 2-0 to the Argentineans. I said to Sheila I can see this going the same way as the game against Germany with Argentina winning by about four goals, praying that I would be wrong.

The game resumed and within 2 minutes Beth Storry had to make a superb save to stop the Argentineans going further ahead. GB started to put more pressure on the Argentineans and broke through their defence. Sarah made a reverse stick shot at goal which was saved, Helen Richardson then struck the rebound which was also saved, but at least GB were now in the Argentina circle and shooting at goal.

Sarah again drove into the circle trying to get a penalty corner and this time she succeeded but again GB failed to finish the routine with a goal.

Further attacks by the Argentinean forwards were all stopped by the fantastic goalkeeping of Beth Storry. GB again managed to get a penalty corner, I said to Sheila, "surely one of these have to go in".

Christa Cullen took the strike which was saved by the goalkeeper, Mel Clewlow then shot at goal from the rebound, which was also saved but the ball came back out, Helen Richardson who was at the top of the circle hit the ball towards the right hand post where Sarah had positioned herself, Sarah deflected the ball into the net at lightning speed, the Argentinean goalkeeper didn't stand a chance of saving it, it was now 2-1, the GB side were elated and all the supporters were screaming for more, this was Sarah's first goal in an Olympic Games. Within 2 minutes GB had another penalty corner which was hit home with speed by Mel Clewlow it was now 2-2, and GB started to play with more confidence and they also looked as if they had more stamina, the Argentineans were starting to run out of steam, although this did not stop them from making further attacks on the GB goal, but once again Beth Storry kept them at bay.

The final whistle went and the game was over, a 2-2 draw between Argentina and Great Britain, this was a fair result because GB played with much more confidence and precision after Sarah scored their first goal, and in my opinion GB coped better with the heat and humidity than the Argentineans did. Tonight Sheila and I would go out and celebrate Sarah's Olympic goal, but before we left the stadium we tried to have a chat with Sarah, but we had to wait whilst the TV crews interviewed her about the game, we managed to have a chat practically shouting from the stand to Sarah on the pitch because due to security we could not get near her, Sheila and I were not use to this, because we always gave Sarah a hug after a game, but this time we had to make do with blowing her a kiss.

Time once again to make our way from the stadium back to our apartment, but at least this time we had some idea of where we were going. Beth Storry's parents Celia and Malcolm had worked out the bus system and were going to show us the way back. The bus came in and we all boarded, I was determined to watch the route of the bus back so that I would know when to get off during the night games when we would be travelling back in the dark, I also counted the stops that the bus made before our destination and was amazed to find that in no time at all we were at the bus station, just a few minutes from our apartment. We said goodbye to Celia and Malcolm but we had already made arrangements to meet them that night for a meal and a few drinks.

Chapter 31

That evening Sheila and I got ourselves ready to meet Malcolm and Celia, we had arranged to meet them by the Marco Polo hotel, we had already selected a Thai restaurant which was only a few minutes' walk from our apartment and also just a few minutes' walk from the Marco Polo hotel.
At about 7.30 PM we met Malcolm and Celia, and we all strolled up to the restaurant, it was a lovely evening, but hot and humid.

The Thai restaurant was really lovely; we were welcomed at the door by ladies in

Thai costume, taken inside and shown to our table.

The setting was superb we had a huge round table for just the four of us, there was a young Thai girl already at our table, she brought us the menus, and just stood there, I then realised, that this young waitress would stay at our table and just serve us throughout our meal.

The menu had a wonderful selection of all Asian dishes, after some discussion we all agreed to try something different, and share the dishes between us, I was going to order a red Thai curry, and that's when we hit the first problem, the waitress couldn't understand a word we were saying, she was very embarrassed, but we were the ones who should have been embarrassed, as we were guests in her country. The waitress went away and came back with the manager, who spoke a little English, and with the help of pointing at the photos in the menu, we eventually ordered our food.

To say the food was amazing would be an understatement, every meal that we had ordered was superb, the service was far superior than any other restaurant that I had ever been in, we had a few bottles of beer to accompany the meals, it had been a splendid end to a very good day, we had seen a great game of hockey with GB playing much better than expected, a great goal from Sarah and now a fantastic meal with excellent company in Celia and Malcolm.

We asked our waitress in some sort of sign language if we could pay the bill, again she didn't understand and went for the manager who did understand what we wanted, and when the bill came I could not believe it, we had had four different meals an accompaniment of rice, quite a few beers, and the total was less than £24 for the four of us, I paid the waitress, and when she brought the change I just gave it all to her, she was quite taken aback, and didn't know what to do, but I just pushed it all into her pocket, to us with all due respect it was peanuts, but to the waitress it was a lot of money. Sheila and I ate at this restaurant many times, and it never failed to impress us, and we nearly always had the same waitress at our table we grew quite fond of her, if she was ever outside at the door welcoming people in to the restaurant, and she saw us pass, she would always give a little discrete wave.

Chapter 32

Wednesday was a rest day for the Great Britain squad, but we had arranged to meet Sarah at about 4 o'clock that afternoon at the GB Lodge, so we had quite a few hours to do what we wanted, Sheila wanted to go to a place called the Pearl market, a massive shopping outlet that sold everything you could think of, very cheaply but mostly counterfeit.
We made our way to the main street where all the taxi cabs were, stopped off for some breakfast, and then hailed a cab; the market was about a twenty minute drive away.
Now we had been warned about the way the taxi drivers drove but I could not believe it, my heart was in my mouth, at one point he nearly crashed three times in the same spot and one of those were whilst he was stopped, the traffic in Beijing is really heavy and there are cars,

lorries and busses all coming at you from different directions. I was not sorry to get out of that taxi; only thing was I knew we had to get into another one to get back to our apartment.

Sheila was in her element at the Pearl market with shopping being one of her hobbies, but I was fed up after about fifteen minutes. There were thousands of people there, you could not move and the noise and bustle was immense and every stall you passed they tried to drag you in to buy something, I was beginning to think the taxi ride wasn't so bad.

On the top of the Pearl market was a huge restaurant, so Sheila and I made our way there to have some lunch, it was heaven, the food was very good, it was quiet and you had great views over Beijing. Sheila said she wanted to buy a few more gifts, and then we headed back to our apartment.

Due to the heat and humidity, it was another shower and change of clothes; thank God the apartment had air conditioning. It was already time to get another cab to take us down to the GB Lodge to see Sarah, our time in Beijing was getting easier by the minute, we now knew where to get the taxi's, and where to get out by the lodge.

It was great to see Sarah and give her the hugs, that we had wanted to give her after her game against Argentina, she was really pleased that she had scored, and she said that all the girls felt more confident after that game.

Sarah only had one hour to stay with us, and this went very quickly, next thing we knew she was being called to get the bus back to the Olympic Village, we hugged and kissed her again, telling her we would see her tomorrow for the game against New Zealand. This game would start at nine o'clock in the evening, another late night lay ahead. We waved Sarah off, said goodbye to a few other parents at the lodge telling them we would see them the following night, then made our way outside, we were stopped by security who told us there was a large demonstration going on outside and that we were to take our identity badges off, we were also told that once we were outside the gates to turn right and not to stop for anyone.

The guards opened the gates of the Lodge to let us out and what we saw was very alarming, there were hundreds of demonstrators outside all chanting and scuffling with a very high contingency of police. We turned right has we had been told and walked right into a team of police carrying a stretcher with another policeman bleeding quite heavily on it. The demonstration was all to do with problems between China and Tibet, and the demonstrators were using the Olympic Games as their platform to get publicity. Sheila and I were very glad to get away from there and hoped that there would not be a repeat of it.

We managed to get a taxi in all the furore, showed the driver the card for the Marco Polo hotel and off we went. The driver dropped us off right outside the entrance to the hotel; we were both still quite shaken up after our experience, so I said to Sheila shall we go in the Hotel and have a few drinks to calm us down. The inside of the Hotel was beautiful compared to our apartment, and we settled down in to some really comfortable chairs, the waiter took our order, and

164

within minutes we were starting to relax with our drinks, I had two drinks and Sheila had one, the bill came to over twenty five pounds, if you want comfort and elegance you have to pay for it. I said to Sheila "I think we shall stick to our lovely Thai restaurant", and that night that's where we again dined.

Chapter 33

Thursday the 14th of August 2008, GB was to play New Zealand at 21.00 hours or 9 o'clock at night in old money. The advantage being it was a lot cooler because the day had been very hot and humid once again.
All the parents took their seats awaiting the start of the match, I get butterflies in my stomach before every game, and it's the anticipation of the outcome of the match that affects me.

The game started quietly with both teams playing with a little trepidation, GB really needed to win this game and there was only one place separating both sides in the world rankings, so it wasn't going to be easy.

For the first twenty minutes both sides moved the ball around the pitch hoping for a mistake from their opponents to let them through the defence and try and get that opening goal. In the 29th minute New Zealand scored from a penalty corner 1-0 to the Blacksticks, play restarted and almost immediately GB attacked the New Zealand goal, and great play from Alex Danson saw the ball hit the back of the net, the teams were back on equal footing, it was now 1-1. With just seconds to go for the end of the first half GB scored again with Ann Panter slotting the ball home, but the umpire decided the ball was played to high, and disallowed the goal.

The second half started and again GB attacked the New Zealand goal only being denied by superb goal keeping from the New Zealand goalkeeper, but after just fifteen minutes play, GB scored again from a penalty corner, hammered home by Crista Cullen, the score stood now as 2-1 to GB. There were no further goals and it was a well deserved win for Great Britain

and winning the match put them on equal
points as Japan, who GB would face next,
on Saturday.

Once again we made our way to the bus
station to make the now short journey
back to our apartment, we said goodnight
to Malcolm and Celia Storry, saying we
would see them at the next game on
Saturday.
It was a lovely night still very warm and
humid as we walked from our stop at the
bus station and looking at the main
Olympic arena the Birds Nest all lit up
was fantastic, there were a lot of people
still milling around, even at that time of
night. Sheila and I were getting the usual
amount of stares from the Chinese people
and the children looked at us in
amazement. We decided not to go straight
back to our apartment, but to go for a walk
down to the centre where all the main
restaurants were, it would have been nice
if there was such a thing as a pub were we
could finish off the night with a glass of
wine but that was not to be, so we just
walked around for a while soaking up the
beautiful Chinese atmosphere, then made

our way back to our apartment, we were saluted by the young guards on the gate as we entered the grounds of where our apartment was situated, they were now getting used to seeing these two strange Europeans coming and going at all different times.

Back in our apartment the room was really cool thanks to the air conditioning, we settled down for a good night's sleep. Tomorrow we were going back down to the GB Lodge to meet Sarah for an hour or so, Sheila and I really looked forward to those meetings where we could chat privately and give her a nice few hugs, and to let her know how well she was playing and coping with the extreme heat and humidity.

We awoke on Friday morning to another very hot day. After showering and changing, we walked down to the centre for a breakfast of coffee and pastries. We had a few hours to kill before meeting Sarah at the Lodge, so we walked around the shops, even before noon the heat was exhausting, and it was not long before we found ourselves in a lovely little sandwich bar having a long cold drink.

Sheila and I had decided to make our way down to the GB Lodge a little earlier so that we could have a look around down there, so that's what we did, we hailed yet another taxi and I must be honest I feared for my life every time we travelled in one. Once again by using hand signals we managed to guide the driver to where we wanted to go, we stopped the taxi a little way from the lodge so that we could walk around and take in the sights of this area. In this area was the aquatics centre where all the swimming and diving competitions were held, there were hundreds of people walking about. There were police road blocks set up here there and everywhere, where they would stop the traffic to allow a coach with Olympic Athletes on, clear access to wherever they were going, it was truly amazing.

After walking around for a while the heat and humidity once again got to Sheila and I, so we made our way to the lodge, after signing in we were grateful for the lovely cool and calm feeling of the Lodge after the hustle and bustle outside. Sarah arrived around 2 o'clock. Whereas some of the GB hockey team would come in looking down in the dumps and as if they had the weight of the world on their shoulders, Sarah would always come in cheerful and smiling, not only was her Olympics going really well but she was enjoying every moment of it, and intended to make the most of it.

Sarah told us that after the game with New Zealand they had had their management meetings then they were free and as there was no game the following day a few of the girls had found some bicycles, and rode around the Olympic Village until the early hours of the morning, chatting to other Olympic Athletes from all over the world she said it was surreal.

Once more our time with Sarah was up it had gone so quickly yet again. One of the management team would come in to tell the athletes, that their coach was outside and they were once more whisked back to the Olympic Village. We would now see Sarah on Saturday when GB played against Japan.

Chapter 34

Today's game against Japan was to be played a little earlier at 20.30 in the evening, this was still an advantage because although once again it was very warm and humid, you didn't have that intense searing heat that you had during the day.

This was another very important game for GB, if they could win this there was still a chance of a semi-final place.

Like all games each side starts off tentatively, sizing each other up, and then making the all important attack and this was the case for GB in the 6th minute they attacked the Japanese goal but the failure of the GB forwards to complete the attack, begs the question, were they up to the job in my humble opinion some of them were not.

Sarah was running her heart out giving everything she had, making some superb runs up the right wing and then passing the ball hard and accurate into the circle where again the forwards were failing to connect with the ball to score.

Thirty two minutes into the game Ann Panter scored for GB; it was 1-0 to GB at

half time. The start of the second half saw
Japan attack the GB goal time after time
but thanks to some superb goalkeeping by
Beth Storry, they were not able to
capitalise on their attacks. Chloe Rogers
received a yellow card in the 47th minute
and was sent off; Japan tried to take
advantage of the numerical difference but
was unable to break down the GB
defence. In fairness to Japan their
determination paid off with a fine penalty
corner in the 60th minute giving them the
equaliser, with just ten minutes to go it
was 1-1. It looked as if both teams would
take one point each from the game but in
the dying seconds a cleverly worked
penalty corner saw Crista Cullen scoring
the winning goal with no chance of Japan
replying, time had run out. GB were very
worthy winners of this game, the Japanese
were devastated, as a team they broke
down and cried, they were all on their
knees sobbing their hearts out. Being a
spectator watching this was very
unpleasant, and our hearts went out to
them. One of the Japanese players Kaori
Chiba was actually playing hockey at the
time for Rotterdam in the same squad as

Sarah, and it was lovely to see Sarah leave the GB squad on the pitch and take time to console Kaori. The three points put GB in third place behind Argentina in the pool table; they now had to beat the USA in their final pool game for a chance of reaching the semi-finals. It was going to be a lot to ask. The USA were a very strong side, and GB had sustained quite a few injuries to some key players, and the heat and humidity that they had been playing in for the past week was starting to take its toll.

For us it was back to the cool of the apartment, a few drinks and then bed. Tomorrow Sheila and I were going on a tour that Sarah had arranged for us to the Great Wall of China; we were both very excited about going to see one of the 7 wonders of the world, fantastic.

Chapter 35

Sunday the 17th of August 2008 will stick in my mind forever; it was the day that we were going on a tour to the Great Wall of China. It was an early start for us as we had to meet the coach outside the Marco

Polo hotel at 10 o'clock. It was a whole day tour which included a visit to a monastery, then lunch, enroute to the Great Wall.

The monastery was beautiful with superb statues lovely gardens and was so peaceful; mind you the usual souvenir stalls were already set up. The next part of the tour was lunch at an authentic Chinese restaurant. I don't know how authentic it was, but it was huge there must have been a thousand tourists all eating there at the same time. The food was good but with so many people all talking at the same time it was very noisy, not a part of the tour that I can say I enjoyed. After lunch we had some time to look around yet more stalls selling souvenirs.

The last part and the best part of the tour was the Great Wall of China, it was unbelievable, it was so well organised. As you can imagine again there were hundreds of people there, but the queuing was kept to the minimum, due to the fact that it was very hot at this time of the day. Standing on one of the 7 wonders of the world the Great Wall of China was amazing, having only seen this magnificent spectacle on television and in pictures does nothing for the reality of it, Sheila and I were both determined to walk as far as we could given the heat and humidity, it was not easy or for the faint hearted but we did it, and it's something we will treasure forever, thank you so much Sarah for that experience.

After walking the Great Wall, we felt we needed a short break and some really cold water. I bought a couple of bottles of water, and then we found a lovely shaded garden with some very welcome benches. Sheila and I sat down, took a very long drink of water and relaxed after the strenuous exercise that we had just had. My legs felt quite heavy after our walk, but after a few minutes of sitting down they were coming back to normal. There were quite a number of Chinese families also in the garden and again they were looking at us with some curiosity, a few were even pointing us out to their friends. There were three young Chinese girls just to the left of us, they were looking at us and then talking amongst themselves.

Sheila turned to me and said "They want their photo taken with us", I said "don't be daft", but then one of the girls came over, spoke in Chinese but we got the drift of what she was saying, "could they have their photo taken with us" , how could we refuse, they were such lovely polite people. The three girls then took turns of sitting down with us and having a picture taken, but this opened the flood gates because when the rest of the Chinese people saw what was happening, they wanted a picture taken with us also. Sheila and I found it quite amusing; we know now how all those celebrities feel, and also somewhere all over China, there are framed pictures in houses of families on holiday, with Sheila and I sat in the middle of them.

It was time to leave the Great Wall of China, and make our way back to Beijing, the coach was cool, and the drive back was very relaxing, until we reached the outskirts of the city. The traffic was horrendous; there were jams everywhere, with cars, buses, lorries and taxies all trying to get on the same stretch of road. Eventually after what seemed like hours we were dropped off back at the Marco Polo hotel and after a very long hot and strenuous day we needed to get back to our apartment and take a long shower. After showering and changing we left our apartment to go somewhere for food. When we got outside, we could not believe how hot and humid it was, and smog had come down which made it quite difficult to breath, this was the Beijing smog, which everyone had talked about prior to the Olympic Games starting. Scaremongers had said it would ruin the Games. It was the first time for us to experience it and I must be truthful, if this smog had occurred more frequently, then it could have ruined the Games, because for us, we were having difficulty breathing. I couldn't imagine an athlete running or doing any strenuous exercise in it. We were just praying that the smog would have dispersed by the following day for Sarah's next match.

Having eaten we made our way back to our apartment. If anything the smog was worse. A lot of the Chinese people we passed were wearing face masks to protect them from the smog, it was only a short distance back to the apartment, and we were glad to get back inside. After a long but fantastic day, we were going to have an early night, Sheila and I were both exhausted, and soon we were both in a deep sleep.

Chapter 36

Sheila and I had awoken to find another very hot day but the good thing was, is that the smog had gone, leaving a beautiful sunny sky.
Today was a very important day for Great Britain in their game with the USA, anything but a win would be deemed as a failure.
The game was due to start at 18.00 hrs, Sheila, myself and the rest of the British supporters were seated waiting for the game to start. It was still very hot and humid and I felt for the GB squad who were going to have to run around for the next seventy minutes in that heat.

Looking up towards the sky I could see the usual helicopters circling the Hockey Arena. They did this security check before every game started. It made you aware that they took the threats of certain groups of people that they were going to try and disrupt the Olympic Games, as serious.

The GB squad were doing their usual pre-game warm up on the pitch, some of the GB supporters were chanting, GB, GB, Sarah looked up and raised her stick. Sheila and I knew although she could not see us from where she was that the raised stick was a wave to us.

The match started with the very strong USA attacking as soon as the whistle was blown, the onslaught was defended well and thanks again to brilliant goal keeping by Beth Storry, the USA were denied from taking the lead. The USA had their first penalty corner in the eighth minute which they failed to capitalise on, but within minutes they had another penalty corner but they failed to control the strike and GB were able to breathe a sigh of relief.

GB was trying to get on terms with the USA but either due to the heat, or that they were starting to show fatigue after all the games they had played, they looked as if they were struggling. Sarah was still running her heart out; her arms were glistening with perspiration, which accentuated the muscle tone of her upper arms.

The USA side looked as if they were a lot bigger than the GB girls, and they were very rough, there was a lot of pushing and shoving on the ball and a lot more off the ball out of the view of the umpires. We could see that Sarah was getting battered, whenever she picked up the ball and started to run, the Americans would stop her by fair means or foul. They were very aware of how dangerous she was when she picked up the ball, and in my opinion, the USA team had been pre-told to stop her by any means.

In total the USA team had seven penalty corners during the first half but failed to score even once, I bet the coach wasn't pleased with that. The second half was pretty much the same with the USA being the more dominant side, but still failing to score. GB came back on a number of occasions and looked as if they could score, if they could only get a set piece together. Chloe Rogers and Rachel Walker both made great attempts in front of the goal but it wasn't to be. The match finished as a 0-0 draw, exactly what GB didn't want. The USA had had ten penalty corners during the game and failed to put any of them away, that's very poor hockey.

Sarah commented after the game that although she thought GB had played as well as they could against a very tough team, it was the USA's physical toughness that wore them down. GB was now chasing for 5th or 6th position and they would know the outcome after playing their next opponents Australia on Friday.

Chapter 37

Today the 22nd of August 2008 would be Sarah's final Olympic game, Sarah had played well throughout the tournament and we were very proud of her. Sarah never gave up in any of the matches; she kept running and kept fighting until the last second of every match unlike some I could mention.

The match started at 11 o'clock and already it was very, very hot. It was going to be really tough on that pitch today for both sides. Both teams were passing the ball around, using as much of the pitch as they could with the ball, rather than running, to conserve energy and reduce the amount of fluid they would lose during this game. GB conceded the first penalty corner after just eleven minutes, this was going to be Australia's first shot on goal, but thanks once again to fantastic goalkeeping by Beth Storry they failed to get the ball into the back of the net. GB played some useful hockey getting the ball into the circle but failing to get any shots at goal on.

In the 29th minute Australia broke through GB's defence and scored a cracking goal, 1-0 to Australia. With just 21 seconds before the half time hooter GB were awarded a penalty corner but the Australian defence were very quick onto the ball and managed to slip the ball out of play. GB now had only 35 minutes in the second half to secure 5th place, could they do it.

During the half time break both teams had taken on plenty of fluid and had ice towels placed around their necks to try and reduced their body temperature due to the excessive heat. When they came back on to the pitch you could see their bodies gleaming with perspiration, the second half was going to be tough for both sides. The game restarted and GB attacked the Australian defence with gusto and within 3 minutes had been awarded a penalty corner. A well worked routine by Ann Panter and Crista Cullen failed to bring the scores level. As supporters we were very disappointed, but there was still plenty of time as long as GB didn't run out of stamina, due to heat exhaustion. In the 45th minute GB again secured a penalty corner, could they score this time? Again Anne Panter took the penalty corner, passed the ball to Mel Clewlow at the top of the circle, Clewlow fed the ball back into the circle, where it was deflected of Ann Panter to Sarah who thumped the ball home into the back of the net, Sheila and I were screaming Sarah had scored her second Olympic goal and at a crucial time. Our joy was short lived because the Australians had asked for the video umpire to check if the goal should be allowed, after what seemed like ages, the video umpire ruled that the goal should be disallowed because the ball went over the legal height for a first shot on goal. We and many other people failed to see anything wrong with Sarah's goal, and thought the decision of the video umpire was not the right one.

The GB team were devastated and rightly so, they tried to come back from their disappointment but their game was suddenly lacking the impetus that they had had. With just 10 minutes to go Australia scored again, but this time it was their goal that was disallowed after another video umpire decision. Danny Kerry decided in the last 5 minutes to take Beth Storry the goalkeeper off, and replace her with another outfield player, and use Crista Cullen as defence and goalkeeper hoping to throw more forwards at the Australian goal but in my opinion it was a huge mistake, because with just 2 minutes to go the Australians scored after Crista

Cullen tried but failed to clear the ball, this in no way reflects on Crista, as she was just under so much pressure, and with far too much work to do. The game ended 2-0 to Australia and GB having to settle for 6th position, which was by no means counted as a failure, they had increased their world ranking by four places.

Once again it was time to head back to our apartment, leaving the Olympic Hockey stadium for the last time, as the following day we were heading back home to Wales. We had one more night to enjoy Beijing, Sheila and I went to our favourite restaurant for our last evening meal, which as usual was superb, we walked around after our meal taking in the sights and sounds which we had now become used to.

We made our way back to our apartment for an early night, as we had to leave by 8 o'clock in the morning for the airport, a taxi had been arranged to pick us up outside, and we didn't want to be late for that.

The flight back home to Great Britain was uneventful, just long and tiring. Back at

Heathrow, we managed to get an earlier coach back to Wales, where Dave and Jane Hopkins would kindly pick us up at the coach station and drive us back to their house where we had left our car.

The final leg of our long journey was just a short drive to our home, by then it was getting quite late, and Sheila and I were both ready to get in to our own bed. After living for two weeks in a stranger, not very comfortable apartment, our home was luxury.

Sheila and I just had one day to relax, before we had to drive back up to London again to meet Sarah on the Monday, when all the Olympic athletes would fly back in to Heathrow Airport from Beijing, in their specially chartered Boeing 747 with the nose cone painted gold, in recognition of all the gold medals won by Team GB.

Chapter 38

On the Sunday night prior to our trip back up to London Sarah sent me a text telling me where to meet her on the Monday.

The plan was that all the Team GB athletes would be transported by coach from Heathrow Airport to the Runnymede Hotel in Surrey.
This location was to be kept secret so that the athletes could meet up with their family and friends without being hassled by the press; Sarah also gave me a code word to use when we arrived at the Runnymede Hotel.

On the Monday morning, Sheila and I made our way up to the Hotel in Surrey. As we approached the hotel, there was a line of cars at the barrier to the entrance of the hotel, with two very large security guys stopping the cars. As I approached the barrier I wound my window down, and this fierce looking but very polite security guy asked me my business at the hotel, I just gave the codeword, he said "have a good day sir" and lifted the barrier for me to drive on.
Inside the hotel we were guided to a room where all the other family and friends were. The only press allowed into the hotel were the BBC, who was also at Heathrow Airport awaiting the arrival of

the jet with Team GB on. The BBC had erected large TV screens around the room so that we all could watch the progress of the last stages of the jet landing bringing the athletes home.

After a while word came through to the commentator with the BBC who was with us, that the Boeing jet was in sight, the TV pictures went back to Heathrow, and we all cheered when we saw the beautiful sight of the jumbo jet with its gold nosecone, on final approach to Heathrow Airport.

It was surreal watching that plane coming into land knowing Sarah was on it having been part of the one thing she had always wanted, being an Olympian.

The plane landed, and taxied to the VIP area, where normally only Royalty arrive. There was a mass of photographers and press awaiting the athletes to get the first pictures of them, on their return to Great Britain. The doors finally opened after what seemed like an age. Sheila and I had our eyes glued to the TV screen to catch our first glimpse of Sarah, again after what seemed like a lifetime we saw Sarah emerge through the cabin doors, as usual Sarah was laughing, even after that long journey, she was still full of life.

As the athletes came down the plane steps, the athletes who had won gold, silver or bronze medals were being interviewed by the press, it was such a proud moment for all of the family and friends watching in that room.

Gordon Brown the then Prime Minister was also meeting the athletes as they came off the plane, we watched as Sarah shook hands with him, then disappeared from view, as she went inside the VIP terminal.

After about one hour the first of the coaches carrying the athletes from Heathrow to the Runnymede Hotel arrived. Sheila and I were waiting in anticipation to see Sarah and give her a welcome home hug. We watched as one then two then three coaches arrived and went, but as the fourth coach came in we could see Sarah, again laughing and joking with her team mates. Sarah came off the coach as if she had just played a game of hockey for one of her old teams, not having come back from an Olympic

Games. Sheila and I both had tears in our eyes when we met Sarah, we were so glad to see her back safe, and also I can't put in to words how proud we were of her.

There was a garden party being held for the returning athletes at the Runnymede, this was held in the hotel grounds right on the banks of the river Thames. It was fantastic, seeing all the athletes together for the first time, Sheila and I met some wonderful people that day; it really was a treasured moment.

Finally it was time to say goodbye to everyone, and for me to drive back home to Wales again. Lorries had turned up at the Runnymede, with all the athletes luggage on board, it took quite a while before we found Sarah's luggage and loaded it into our car, but getting away was not going to be easy, team mates and athletes we didn't know kept coming up to Sarah to say goodbye, and to have just one more photograph taken. I said to Sarah that we needed to get going so that we wouldn't be that late arriving home, as the following day Sarah had to be in Cardiff with the other ten Welsh Olympic athletes

190

for a tour of the city in an open top bus, tomorrow was going to be another busy day.

Eventually we departed the Runnymede Hotel, but by now word had got around, that all the Olympic Athletes were at the hotel, and the road out of the Runnymede was lined with public well wishers, who were waving and cheering at us as we drove by. They could see Sarah sitting in the back of the car with her GB kit on, Sarah loved it and waved back. Once we reached the motorway, Sarah told us of the party like atmosphere that was on the plane bringing the athletes home. Sarah was tired but the excitement of it all was keeping her going, but she did manage to drop off to sleep in the back of the car on our way up the M4 motorway.

Chapter 39

Today Sarah would take part in an open top bus tour of Cardiff, with the other Welsh athletes of Team GB.
Sheila was very disappointed because she couldn't get the time off work to come to

Cardiff for this memorable occasion, so Sarah dressed again in her Team GB tracksuit would only have me for company. I drove Sarah to a hotel in Cardiff Bay where she met the rest of the athletes, and was informed of the tour plan.

The bus would tour the city where thousands of fans would be lining the roads, cheering and waving Welsh flags, the bus would finish up at the Welsh Assembly building, where the athletes would be met by the first minister and other dignitaries.

I was amongst the crowds of people waiting for the bus to appear and when it did a roar went up like I have never heard before, the crowd were cheering, waving flags and banners, it was a fantastic moment to see our daughter up there on that bus waving back to the crowds of people.

Sheila missed that moment only because somebody who didn't have children and no compassion wouldn't give her a few hours off work.

After a meet and greet session in the Welsh assembly, where Sarah was interviewed by a number of TV and press reporters on her experience of the Olympics, Sarah said she was hungry, so we left the assembly building to find somewhere to eat, "this will do" Sarah said, "I will have a Pizza in here". As we walked in to the restaurant all the people who were already in there looked up, and saw Sarah in her Team GB tracksuit, and I could see they were saying to each other, she must be an Olympic Athlete. It didn't bother Sarah though, she just ate her Pizza, and when the waiter came and said congratulations to Sarah, she just thanked him.

Sheila had to wait until the evening news to see Sarah tour in the open top bus, a moment missed but at least thanks to the reporting of it by the TV companies; she did get to see her.

As I have said before Sarah takes everything in her stride, she is not bothered by anything and if there is a hill to climb she will climb it.

Whatever Sarah needed to do to get to these Olympic Games she did without question or fuss.

Sarah wasn't born with a silver spoon in her mouth; everything she has achieved has been through shear hard work, determination and guts. Both Sheila and I are so proud of her achievements, not just the Olympic Games although that is the pinnacle of her hockey career, but also the University degree that she worked so hard for. I believe that whatever Sarah sets out to do in life, she will achieve and do well at it.

Sarah stayed home in Wales with us for about three weeks after the Olympic Games, to relax and recover. The hockey season back out in Rotterdam was about to start, and after three weeks of not playing hockey Sarah was starting to miss it. It was time once again for our beautiful Daughter to leave Wales and go back to Holland and start another season with her Rotterdam team mates.

It has always been sad for Sheila and I waving Sarah off each time, you would think we would have become use to it by now, but as a parent I don't think you ever do. We would not see Sarah now until she came home in December for Christmas, but we would follow every game she played out in Holland, on the internet. Our phone bill also takes a steep upward climb when she is in Rotterdam, but it's worth it just to hear her voice.

Chapter 40

In 2005 Great Britain was awarded the 2012 Olympic Games, this is a fantastic achievement for Great Britain and all its athletes. The games are going to cost billions of pounds in what we find now are difficult times, but in my opinion it will be worth it.

This book finishes off really where it started, an athlete, an Olympic Games coming up. Sarah was only the third Welsh Hockey player to go to an Olympic Games, and the first outfield player ever to go.
Sarah has moved back from Rotterdam and is currently training with the GB hockey squad once again, at Bisham

Abbey, for the 2012 Olympics. Will Sarah be the first ever Welsh Hockey player to have played in two successive Olympic Games, watch this space.

London 2012 Olympics

Chapter 1

After the 2008 Beijing Olympic Games, Sarah moved back to Rotterdam, where she renewed her contract with Rotterdam Hockey club for another two years. At this time Sarah did not have any intention of going to try for the London 2012 Olympics.
Sarah once again settled down in Rotterdam, in a new location. Having been given a city apartment as part of her

new contract with Rotterdam. Sarah had
also been supplied with a brand new car.
Sarah's routine became the same, training
once or twice during the week with the
league game of hockey on the Sunday.
After a couple of months of this routine
Sarah was getting bored. In a conversation
I had with her she told me she needed to
do something more than train, and play
hockey for Rotterdam. Sarah told me that
she had had an idea to start a company as
a personal trainer, and after bouncing
some ideas off us and her friends, Sarah
started her personal training company,
called Fitness 18.

 With help from some very good friends
out in Rotterdam she soon had her own
website up and running, and had put out
hundreds of flyers through doors and
business units in Rotterdam and the
surrounding areas. The total cost of setting
up the company and for getting the flyers
made, was just over £500. I told Sarah that
it was worth the money, and if it failed,
she had not lost that much cash.

At first like any new business, she was
having quite a few enquiries, but no
definite customers. This soon changed.

Sarah called us one evening to say that she had signed up her first customer or clients as she liked to call them.

The client wanted Sarah to get his son fit enough to take the police fitness test which would enable him to join the Dutch police force. He also took out the same package for his wife, why he did that was beyond us.

The business went from strength to strength, and soon Sarah had more than enough clients. On some days when she was training with Rotterdam, she would also have to fit in training four clients throughout the day. I think for her clients, having an Olympian as your personal trainer, was more of an ego trip than really being keen on getting fit. As with everything that Sarah does, if she gives 110 per cent, then she would expect her clients to do the same. She would tell her clients, "you pay me to get you fit and to lose weight, and that's what is going to happen".

Sarah was now probably the happiest we had seen her in a long time. She was more occupied, and her business was doing extremely well. At Rotterdam Hockey club though, things were changing.

The club had taken on a new coach for the senior first team, and a lot of the older more experience players had left for more lucrative contracts with other clubs. These changes were showing in the outcome of the games being played at the weekends. Rotterdam had started losing games that the previous season, they were winning, and Sarah was getting frustrated. She had meetings with the clubs owners and told them straight, that the coach was not up to the job. If the club did not spend more money on getting new and more experience players, Rotterdam would slip from the league they were in.

During this time, a number of people associated with GB hockey, had been in touch with Sarah, asking her if she still had any interest, in going for the London 2012 Olympics. Sarah expressed her concerns that having not been involved with the GB team full time as were the hockey players now based at Bisham Abbey, how they would feel if she did decide to come back and go for the Olympics. Sarah was told that they are all professionals, and would accept her, because they knew she had been keeping up the work of staying extremely fit, and she was still playing first class hockey, out in Holland.

Sarah told the GB hockey people, that she was due home for Christmas, December 2010, and would make a final decision then.

Sheila and I knew nothing of these discussions which were taking place between Sarah, and GB hockey. As far as we knew, the London 2012 Olympics, was dead in the water as far as Sarah was concerned.

During her Christmas break with us, Sarah came to me and said "Dad do you think I should go for the 2012 Olympics". I was quite taken aback, as this was the first time Sarah had mentioned it, but as soon as I heard the words 2012 Olympics my heart skipped a beat.

Sheila, Sarah and I then sat down, and Sarah told us about the discussions she had been having with GB hockey, and about her coming back to train at Bisham abbey.

Without showing Sarah, Sheila and I were elated at this news. I said to Sarah, "Not many people would have a second chance of being asked back into the squad, and I think you should grab the opportunity in both hands". Sheila then told Sarah that to play in an Olympic games in your own country, would be every athletes dream, and if the chance is there take it.

So it was decided in December 2010 that if Sarah was given the opportunity, she would come back in to the fold at Bisham Abbey with the GB hockey squad. During the course of the next few weeks Sarah was told that she was welcome to come back to Bisham and start training full time once again with the GB squad.

Having finished her contract with Rotterdam Hockey Club, Sarah returned to the UK in May 2011. The Great Britain hockey squad are based at Bisham Abbey and train together on a daily basis six days per week.

Once again Sarah had to find somewhere to live close enough to Bisham, so that she could travel back and fore daily.

After searching the local areas, Sarah was lucky enough to find a place to live in the beautiful town of Henley On Thames. Sarah would be sharing a property with two other Olympic hopefuls, both who were rowers. The house had been totally renovated and Sarah had a superb room at the top of the house, with her own en-suite bathroom. Sarah was also lucky that she was just a few minutes' walk from the town centre, and just a short stroll to the scenic views of the river Thames. Bisham Abbey, was just a ten minute drive away, perfect.

Although Sarah did not move back permanently to the UK until May 2011, she had been travelling back and forth from Rotterdam mostly on a weekly basis, from early January 2011. Sarah would play her Sunday league game with her club Rotterdam in the morning, and then fly on the Sunday evening to London. Training was at Bisham from the Monday to Thursday. Sarah would then fly back to Rotterdam, for training on the Friday evening. Play Sunday league hockey, before once again boarding a plane to fly back to London for training at Bisham on Monday.

This had been a very hectic time for Sarah and we were overjoyed when she finally settled in Henley on Thames.

Chapter 2

It was now time for Sarah to settle back in to a daily routine of training at Bisham Abbey.

Sarah was very aware that it would take a little while for the rest of the squad, who had been training together for a long time at Bisham to accept her back in to the squad fully. Sarah just kept her head down, got on with all the training and in a matter of weeks; it was as if she had never been away from Bisham.

Once again as a family, we were all settled into a new routine. Sarah training daily at Bisham Abbey, and every few weeks Sheila and I would again make the trip up the M4 to visit Sarah at Henley.

We would stay at a hotel in Henley, and on Sarah's day off from training, we would either go shopping or have a very nice lunch down by the river. Lunch on the river at Henley-On Thames is perfect.

Chapter 3

With the London 2012 Olympics now just over a year away, training at Bisham was constant. There was also a lot of foreign travel coming up for the GB squad. They would be travelling to a lot of countries, playing against teams they would play against in the actual Olympic Games. Also there were a lot of foreign teams travelling to the UK to play against GB at Bisham Abbey.
Teams from Australia, China and Korea just to name a few. They were coming to see how the GB team was progressing. And the way that most of the games were going in GB's favour, they knew that GB was now a formidable force.

In the following months Sarah spent a lot of time abroad. Sheila and I would travel up to see Sarah at Henley and on the rare occasions when Sarah had some free time she would travel home to Wales. It was never for more than a day or so, and to be honest we were not seeing her as much as we would have liked. Sheila and I knew the commitment that was needed for Sarah to be selected for the forth coming Olympics, and had to accept the situation.

Chapter 4

The date for the naming of the GB hockey squad was once again going to be announced on Sheila's birthday the 18th of June 2012. For some reason it was changed after the hockey test event at the Olympic park to the 10th of May 2012. In my opinion this was much better, this would give the 16 chosen players a better chance to gel totally as a team before the Olympic Games.
Again on the 10th of May Sheila and I were on tenterhooks, waiting for the phone call at 9 o'clock from Sarah, telling us if she had been selected or not. We had not had much sleep during the night, and we were both a little edgy.

When the phone rang and Sarah told us that once again she had been selected to go to her second Olympic Games, we were overjoyed. We were not allowed to tell anyone until it was officially announced on the 18th of May.

GB Hockey announced the names of the squad to play at the London 2012 Olympics at the stock exchange in London, on the 18th of May 2012. It was great to see Sarah and her team mates on the TV at news time, all smiling and happy. They all knew they had a huge task ahead of them.

Playing at an Olympic Games in your own country puts a lot more pressure on the athletes to do well in my opinion, but Sheila and I knew that Sarah would cope.

Although Sarah was extremely pleased that she had been selected, there was a lot of sadness for the players who this time had not been chosen. It was difficult for her to see friends that she had trained and played with so upset. The players who had not been selected, were still expected to train with the 16 players who had been selected. This was because if one of the selected players was so badly injured that they could not take part in the Olympics, then one of the unselected players would be able to take their place.

On June the 6th 2012 another test event was going to take place at Chiswick in London, the Investec Cup. Investec, were one of the main sponsors of GB Hockey. Sheila and I had once again made arrangements, to go and watch Sarah and the GB squad in action at this event. On Friday the 25th of May 2012, disaster struck. Sarah phoned us and she was sobbing, apparently whilst playing a friendly match against South Africa, Sarah badly sprained her ankle.

The medical team at GB Hockey had already started treatment on Sarah's ankle. Now it was a race against time to get her fit again, for the Olympic Games.

Just a week before the ankle injury, Sarah had had a nasty knock to her knee which required 6 stitches. The plan now was for Sarah to have a MRI scan on her ankle on the Monday. This would allow the swelling on her ankle to subside a little over the weekend. Sarah would then see the doctor on Monday evening. The doctor would give her the news, whether the injury was too bad or not to get her fit in time. The doctor would also remove the stitches from the cut on her knee at the same time.

Chapter 5

The weekend had really dragged for Sheila and me. We were so concerned for Sarah; having got this far to get to her second Olympics, and now there was a chance that it would all be taken away from her.
We can only praise the medical team at Bisham for their efforts to get Sarah fit again. Emma the GB physiotherapist did a remarkable job. Emma started the treatment required straight away on the Friday when Sarah had the injury, and continued throughout the weekend. Sarah was now on crutches, and given a cast to try and reduce the swelling.

On the Monday Sheila and I drove up to Bisham to see Sarah. We wanted to be with her when she received the news in the evening, on how bad the ankle injury was. If it was too bad to get her fit in time Sarah would be devastated.

It was strange seeing Sarah hobbling about on crutches, this was the first time that she had had an injury of this kind in all the years that she had been playing. Emma the physio was taking Sarah at 3 o'clock for the MRI scan. The doctor was going to see Sarah at 5 o'clock to give her the results. Sheila and I had a few hours of agonising waiting to do.

Throughout all of this I have to say, Sarah was very positive. Not at any time did she say she would not be playing at the Olympics, although it did cross my mind.

Sarah came back from having the MRI scan and at 5 o'clock she went with Emma in to see the doctor. After a while I received a text message from Sarah, I was dreading opening up the message. It just said "not as bad as expected". It was a huge relief to Sheila and me. When Sarah came hobbling back out with a big smile on her face, it said it all.

I asked Sarah what was the result, she said "torn ligaments and some bruising". The treatment would continue, and she would be back in the gym in a few days to keep the upper body strength going. She just had to rest the ankle as much as possible and not put any weight on it. The stitches in her knee had also been removed and Sarah said that she had not felt a thing, tough as old boots these hockey girls.

Sheila and I thanked Emma the physio for all the effort she had put in for Sarah. We then took Sarah home.

Whilst I cooked Sarah a meal, Sheila did a spot of cleaning in Sarah's room because with the crutches, Sarah had not been able to do anything since the day of the injury.

We said our goodbyes to Sarah, telling her to take care and keep in touch. We then headed back up the M4 to our home. What a difference driving home, far more relaxed than when we drove up in the morning.

We now knew that Sarah would not take part in the next test event, the Investec Cup. I must say we were both a little disappointed, but it could have been worse, we could have missed an Olympic Games.

Chapter 6

The outstanding work from the medical and physiotherapy staff at Bisham Abbey soon had Sarah off the crutches, and back into training. Obviously light training at first, but soon she was back playing hockey. After missing a few weeks of playing hockey, it was going to be a big test on Sarah's ankle when the GB squad next played a friendly match. It was to be against South Africa the same team they played when Sarah sustained the injury. Sarah told us, that prior to the match, she had been a little apprehensive, but throughout the game her ankle had caused no problems.

The intensive training continued at Bisham Abbey with now only the sixteen named players for the Olympics having the full attention of the coaching staff.

The London 2012 Olympics was now less than a month away. At the beginning of July the GB Hockey squad were taken to Loughborough to be kitted out. Sarah told us that she could not believe the amount of kit each person was given, everything that they would need for the forthcoming Olympics.
They were given, training kit, playing kit, opening ceremony dress, media dress, in fact kit for all occasions.

The opening ceremony for the London 2012 Olympics was now just two weeks away, on the 27th of July. All of our travel arrangements were now sorted. Sarah would be given two tickets for each game she played in, courtesy of GB Hockey. Each ticket came with a travel card for use on the day of the game. This was a fantastic idea because it prevented there being long queues at the tube stations etc.

The only disappointment for Sheila and me was that although we applied early for opening and closing ceremony tickets we failed to get any, so we would have to watch it at home.

On the 18th of July, the GB Hockey squad entered the Olympic village. Sarah phoned to say it was superb; there was everything that you could imagine there for the comfort and relaxation for the athletes.

Chapter 7

July the 27th 2012, at 9 pm the opening ceremony for the London 2012 Olympics would take place. Sheila and I were glued to the TV in anticipation of seeing our wonderful daughter once again walk in to an Olympic stadium, as part of Team GB.

The opening ceremony for the Beijing 2008 Olympics was amazing, and everyone said it could not be beaten but it was. The opening ceremony for London 2012 surpassed it, it was truly amazing. It was exciting, emotional and had everything that an opening ceremony requires, with something for everyone, from the young to the old, no one was left out.

Finally, after a rollercoaster ride of different emotions from the opening ceremony, the Olympic teams from around the world, started to enter the Olympic stadium.

Sheila and I just could not wait for the entrance of Team GB, and after what seemed like a lifetime, they entered the Olympic stadium. The team were waving their Union Jack flags, waving to the crowds, who were cheering them so loudly. It was a really proud moment for us. At first we could not see Sarah because she was on the right hand side as the team came in, but then she moved to the left, and we saw her beaming face. The smile on Sarah's face said it all; she loved every moment of it.

Once all the teams were inside the stadium, it was now time to light the Olympic flame, and to officially start the London 2012 Olympics. Tomorrow, Sheila and I would head up to London, where for the next two weeks; we would watch our daughter Sarah, take part in the greatest sporting show on earth.

Sarah's first hockey match would start at 7 pm on Sunday the 29th of July. Great Britain v Japan, bring it on.

Chapter 8

In this section of the book I will not be going into as much detail regarding the flow of play as I did in the first section of the book. I will just give details of the score line, which players scored and any interesting events that happened during the game.

The game started at 7 pm on Sunday the 29th of July. After the names of both teams were announced and the national anthems played, it was Great Britain who was to start the match, the ball was passed back, and the game commenced.

Sarah had done her usual three jumps in the air as she has always done before the start of a match. Sarah's London 2012 Olympics was under way.

After just seven minutes Alex Danson scored making the score 1-0 to GB. Great Britain looked the more dominant of the two sides from the beginning. After just twenty three minutes GB scored again, and this time it was Sarah that scored the goal. It was now 2-0 to GB.

Great Britain had already beaten Japan in the 2008 Beijing Olympics, and this match looked as if it was going the same way.

Three minutes later and just twenty six minutes into the match Sally Walton scored from a penalty corner. GB were now winning 3-0. The ball always goes back to the centre line for a restart after a goal has been scored, the game restarted and Great Britain were putting Japan under so much pressure that within two minutes GB had scored again thanks to Alex Danson. It was now 4-0 to GB and only twenty eight minutes into the game.

At half time both teams left the pitch for a ten minute break. Would GB continue in the second half with another rush of goals? This was not to be, although GB were still the more dominant of the two sides in the second half Japan managed to hold them off.

With just four minutes to go in the game, GB captain Kate Walsh was hit full force in the face by a Japanese players stick.

Kate fell to the ground and you could see she was in a great amount of pain. The medical team rushed on, and after treating her on the pitch for a while, Kate was helped off the pitch to tremendous applause from the huge 16000 spectators that were in the stadium. The game again restarted but at the final whistle it was still Great Britain 4 Japan 0.

We later spoke to Sarah to congratulate her on a great win and for scoring her first goal of the 2012 Olympics.
Although obviously very pleased at the win, the team were now very concerned for the welfare of Captain Kate Walsh. Kate had apparently had her jaw bone broken by the hit she had taken to her face.
Sarah told us that Kate would have to endure a four hour operation as soon as possible. Although the public were not going to be told how bad Kate's condition was at that time. Obviously Kate's health was first and foremost in people's minds, but for the team it was also a great worry, that they may not have their very

formidable captain taking part in any further games.
We asked Sarah that if she could, to let us know how Kate's condition was at a later time. Our hearts went out to Kate's parents who were in the stadium at the time of her injury, and must have been horrified to have witnessed it.

Chapter 9

The following day Monday the 30th of July was a rest day for the GB hockey team. We again spoke to Sarah who updated us on Kate's condition.
Kate had had a four hour operation, to have a Titanium plate screwed in to her jaw to hold it together. I asked Sarah if Kate would take any further part in this Olympics and she said "at the moment we don't know, but knowing Kate she would do her best to get back on that pitch with her squad".

The next match for GB was against Korea on Tuesday the 31st of July.
How Great Britain would fare without their captain, who we now knew would

not take part in this game at least, we did not know.

The game against the Korean side was not going to be easy. It seems all the Asian teams learn very quickly the way their opponents play.
The match started at 4 pm with almost a full stadium of spectators and as you can imagine the majority of them were supporting Great Britain. The noise when the team came on to the pitch was incredible. Nearly everyone was chanting GB, GB and stamping their feet at the same time. It was awe inspiring.
GB gave the crowd even more to cheer about when Nicola White scored after just five minutes, 1-0 to Great Britain.
Korea was not going to be a push over for GB, and in the 17th minute of the game they scored, it was now 1-1.
GB were awarded a penalty corner and Crista Cullen, a penalty corner specialist, made sure that the ball went into the back of the net. At half time the score was GB 2, Korea 1.
The second half saw another five goals being added to the score sheet. Goals from

Alex Danson, Georgie Twigg and Chloe Rodgers, sealed the win for GB but Korea did manage to score a further two goals in the second half. Full time result 5-3 to Great Britain.

After the game Sarah sent me a text message asking if we could stay around outside the stadium, as she would be able to come out to see us for about ten minutes.
Eventually after waiting for quite some time Sarah came out. Although very pleased with the result, she said "everyone was a little down, due to the injury to Kate, but that they were determined to win, for their captain".
Whilst we were talking to Sarah, I noticed a chap standing around and although he was wearing official accreditation, I still thought he had wanted Sarah's autograph because she had already signed a number of autographs and had posed for a number of photos with waiting fans. What we hadn't realised is, that he was Sarah's "minder" whilst she was outside of the stadium. The chap then came on to Sarah,

and said "just another two minutes Sarah; the press are waiting for you back inside".

We gave Sarah a few more hugs and kisses, and told her we would speak the following day, and see her at the next game which was going to be against Belgium.

Chapter 10

The third game for Great Britain in the London 2012 Olympics was against Belgium. Belgium were newcomers to the Olympics, never having played in an Olympic Games previously.
Although on paper GB should easily beat Belgium, but as in any sport you cannot take anything for granted.
The times of the matches for GB in the preliminary rounds of the tournament were at either 4 pm in the afternoon or at 7 pm in the evening. Today's match against Belgium was at 7 pm.

Having made our way to the Olympic park, then through all the security checks and then finally a twenty five minute walk to the hockey stadium, we were sat in our seats waiting once again for GB to make their appearance on the pitch. Alex Danson ran out onto the pitch and the whole stadium erupted in cheers and clapping. As the rest of the players came on to the pitch for their pre-match warm up the crowded stadium just burst into cheering and chanting. The atmosphere was electric. Mexican waves were going around the stadium from one end to the other. The GB supporters loved every minute of being in the stadium and were determined to enjoy themselves.

As the game began I thought that Great Britain seemed to be holding back against the Belgian side. GB being the more experienced and skilful of the teams, I expected them to take the game more forcefully to the Belgians.
In fairness to the Belgians, what they lacked in skill going forward, they more than made up for it in defence. In my opinion their defence was superb. GB was

throwing everything at the Belgians, trying to break through their defence, but without much success. Then finally just two minutes before half time, Ashleigh Ball scored, 1-0 to Great Britain. It had taken 33 minutes for GB to get the breakthrough they needed, but the game was still there to be won by either side.

Danny Kerry would not have been pleased with his side's performance in the 1st half, and during the half time break would have expressed his feeling to the GB squad. Although the GB squad were still missing their captain Kate Walsh after her dreadful injury sustained in their 1st game against Japan, there was no excuse for their lacklustre performance against this Belgian side.

Great Britain started the 2nd half of the match at far more lively pace, attacking the Belgian goal constantly. This pressure paid off in the 40th minute when Scotland's Laura Bartlett scored for GB. GB 2, Belgium 0. A final goal with just one minute to go from a Crista Cullen penalty corner sealed the game for Great Britain. GB 3, Belgium 0. It had not been

GB's best performance of the tournament so far, but a win is a win, and they were top of the table in their group. The almost packed stadium loved yet another win from GB, and showed their appreciation when the GB squad did their lap of honour by cheering and clapping constantly until the squad left the pitch.

Tomorrow was a rest day for Great Britain, and the next game for them would be against China, silver medallists in the 2008 Beijing Olympics, they would be tough opponents.

Chapter 11

Great Britain had now won three games out of three. If they win the next game against China they would be through to the semi-finals.
The great thing about today's game, was that captain Kate Walsh was back in the squad. I found this absolutely amazing considering just a few days ago Kate had been hit full force in the face with a hockey stick, and had had her jaw broken.

The game commenced at 4.00pm and after about ten minutes I said to Sheila that GB again did not look comfortable playing against China. Whether it was psychological, knowing that China had won the silver medal in the 2008 Olympics, or perhaps after three games, they may have been a little tired, I didn't know.

The one consolation for Sheila and I was that Sarah was having a storming match. Constantly trying to raise the GB side and making some fantastic runs down the right hand wing.

The Chinese defence were amazing, nothing the GB side tried could penetrate that defence, and after 35 minutes at half time the score was 0-0.

Six minutes into the second half China breached the Great Britain defence, and scored the 1st goal of the match. China 1, GB 0.

As much as GB tried to even the score line, with Sarah once again repeatedly attacking the Chinese defence, it was not to be. China then scored again. It was now 2-0 to China.

Great Britain's hopes of winning four out
of four matches was diminishing with
every minute of play. Also the chance of
going straight through to a semi-final was
also disappearing fast.

Finally, with just two minutes of the game
remaining Sarah broke through the
Chinese defence and got a short corner for
GB. With great effort Crista Cullen scored
a fantastic goal, but it seemed like too
little too late in my opinion. The game
ended 2-1 to China.

Just to reiterate this was Kate Walsh's
first game back after receiving that
dreadful injury in the game against Japan
on the first day of play. Kate had to wear a
face mask to protect her from any further
injury. Now you would have thought that
a player back in their first game after such
an injury would be playing with caution. I
can assure you that that was not the case
with Kate; she played without fear, and
was exceptional in defence, a true heroine
in my eyes.

Great Britain was to play the Netherlands
next, and they would now have to either
beat them in that game, or if the results of

later games went GB's way, a draw would do and they would qualify for a semi-final.

The later games did not go GB's way and it seemed now that they would have to beat the Netherlands, to get to the semi-finals.

There was a glimmer of hope in all of this, China were to play Japan on the same day as GB were to play the Netherlands. If Japan could beat China and that was a huge if, because Japan had not beaten anyone so far in this Olympic Games, then win, lose or draw Great Britain would be through to the semi-finals of the Olympic Games. Would lady luck shine on Great Britain we would have to wait and see.

Chapter 12

On Monday the 6th of August 2012, Sheila and I and a few very close friends were invited to the Grange Hotel near St. Paul's cathedral. This was to welcome the parents and close friends of the athlete involved in the Olympic Games. Great Britain hockey had laid out a lovely buffet and drinks for all the family and friends.

Whilst we were all enjoying the buffet, the game against Japan and China had got under way. If Japan could beat China, the result of our game against the Netherlands later would not matter; we would still go through to the semi-finals.
It was very close to half time and neither Japan nor China had scored, Japan still had another thirty five minutes to score in the second half, and with that GB still had a chance of a certain semi-final.

All the family and friends were mingling and chatting around the room, when a roar went up. Japan had scored. It was now 1-0 to Japan, but with another twenty minutes to go, there was still time for China to come back. China would not sit on their laurels, because there was still a chance of a semi-finals place for them also.
I left the room where the buffet was being held, and made my way to the bar area, where the game between Japan and China was being televised.
There was just ten minutes to go and Japan were still winning by that very short margin of one goal. The tension and emotion I was feeling at that time was

immense. With just about two minutes of the game to go, I was talking to myself, saying "come on Japan, keep them out, keep them out". The full time whistle went, and there was another roar from the crowd. Somehow Japan had beaten China 1-0 and with that given Great Britain a road through to a semi-final. Everyone was relieved because now win lose or draw against the Netherlands, we were still going forward to the semi-finals.

You can't get away from the fact that the Netherlands are probably one of the best teams in the world, and would have been very difficult to beat. Although we expected Great Britain to give them a good run for their money, there was now no pressure on GB to have to win. The match against the Netherlands started at 7.00 pm and personally I thought Great Britain was playing the better hockey. The Netherlands who were also through to the semi-finals looked rather nervous, and did not look anything as good as I had seen them in the past. In the 29th minute GB were awarded a penalty corner, and once again Crista Cullen rose to the challenge, and put the ball firmly into the back of the net. At half time it was 1-0 to GB.

The game restarted for the second half, and it looked as if the Netherlands had been given a good talking to during the half time break by their coach because they had started the second half like a different team. Although the GB defence still kept the Netherlands at bay, it now looked as if it was only a matter of time before they scored.

After forty three minutes, the Netherlands were awarded a penalty corner, which they scored from. It was now 1-1, and although GB were still playing really well, they could just not get that 2nd goal. The Dutch side scored again in the 52nd minute making it 2-1 to the Netherlands.

I don't know whether GB would have made a more concerted effort to win this game if the semi-final place had depended on it, I would like to have thought so.

The game ended with the Netherlands winning by 2 goals to 1. It was a good performance by GB in the 1st half, but they did seem to lose control of the game in the 2nd half. Although the outcome of the match made no difference to GB's position in the group standings, it is still always good to win.

We spoke to Sarah later, and she was very happy with her performance against the Netherlands, and in fairness to her, she did have a very good game. So far Sarah had played really well in all of the matches and also had managed to stay out of trouble and not get injured, which is always a godsend.

Sarah told us that they would be playing Argentina next for a place in the final. Argentina are a world class team and would not go down without a fight. GB had beaten them in the past, and I thought that GB could beat them again, especially for a place in an Olympic final.

GB would play Argentina at 8.00 pm on Wednesday the 8th of August 2012. If GB managed to beat Argentina, they would be then playing for an Olympic gold or silver medal; if they lost, they would then play for the bronze medal and Argentina would be playing for gold or silver.

Chapter 13

Sheila and I were in our seats at the Olympic hockey stadium by 7.00 pm for the game against Argentina. The stadium was filling up fast and there would be close to 16000 spectators, most of them cheering on Great Britain.
As usual we were both feeling apprehensive regarding the outcome of the match. A win here for GB would put them into the Olympic final. The Netherlands were already through to the final, and the winner of this match would play them for the Olympic gold medal.

The whistle blew and the first 35 minutes of this match was under way.
Great Britain started off really well showing the Argentineans that they meant business. Within the first few minutes GB had attacked the Argentine goal but was unable to capitulate on it by scoring.
Argentina made a counter attack, and was awarded a penalty corner from which they scored, 1-0 to Argentina.

We knew that once this side got in to the circle they were very dangerous and this goal just proved that.

Although Great Britain were still playing really well they could just not penetrate the Argentine defence and score.

Just 31 minutes into the game Argentina scored again, it was now 2-0 to Argentina. We knew that Danny Kerry would be really critical of some of his players at half time due to the fact that they were giving the ball away to easily. We also knew it was the same players making the same mistakes constantly. In my opinion if you can't stop a ball after four years of training, then you shouldn't be there.

The game restarted, GB now had only 35 minutes to take the lead and win this match. As the clock counted down, the chances of winning were ebbing away. Argentina's defence would not allow the GB side through, and you could see the frustration within the GB side. A superb run from GB's Alex Danson caught the Argentinean defence off guard, and with just 6 minutes remaining on the clock she scored. The score was now 2-1 to

Argentina, would there be enough time remaining for GB to score again. It was a very tough ask but in fairness they did try, throwing everything they had at the Argentine goal. But it was not to be, the full time whistle went, Argentina had won and was through to the final, with the Netherlands.

This is where it gets very difficult as a parent watching your child play in high profile tournaments such as this.

Sarah was on the floor of the pitch breaking her heart; she now knew that a chance of an Olympic gold medal had been taken away from her. Sheila and I had seen her upset in the past after losing certain games but this time she was inconsolable. Crista Cullen was holding Sarah, trying to comfort her. It was really upsetting for Sheila and me.

Great Britain did their usual lap of honour; the supporters were cheering and whistling like crazy, they just loved this GB side

When the GB team came round to the side of the pitch where we were sitting, we waved to Sarah and blew her a kiss but we

could see she was devastated, it was so sad.
After the game, Sheila and I waited outside for over an hour to see Sarah. When Sarah eventually came out, she looked shell shocked. In all the years of watching her play, we had never seen her like this. Nothing we would say or do would ease the pain that she was feeling right now after losing to Argentina, and the place in the final.

The following day, the photo of Crista Cullen consoling Sarah on the hockey pitch made the front page of the London Metro newspaper, with the headline, "don't cry for me Argentina".
After speaking to Sarah that day, we could tell she was really down. I told her there was still a medal to play for, forget the gold or silver, and to go get the bronze medal.
The bronze medal match would be against New Zealand on Friday the 10th of August 2012.
New Zealand had been playing very well indeed and would be tough opponents.
Both sides knew this was the last chance

saloon. Win and you get an Olympic medal, lose and you go home with nothing.

Chapter 14

Friday the 10th of August 2012 was going to be one of the most important days in Sarah's 18 years of playing hockey. Today Great Britain were going to play against New Zealand, for the Olympic bronze medal.
Sheila and I were in our seats by 3.00 pm, the game was due to start at 3.30 pm. We were both praying for a GB win. Sarah had given up so much in life just for this moment in time, to be an Olympic medallist. Sheila and I both knew it would break her heart, if GB failed today, and did not win that bronze medal.

The hockey stadium was a complete sell out with 16000 spectators. The atmosphere was electric, with supporters already chanting, GB, GB.
When the GB players came on to the pitch for their pre match warm up, the stadium exploded. The supporters were clapping,

cheering and stamping their feet. The noise was amazing.

The ball was pushed back and the game for the Olympic bronze medal had started. The only disappointment for us was that Danny Kerry had not started Sarah, which was a complete mystery, considering that she was probably one of the most consistent players throughout the Olympic tournament.

We also knew that Sarah would not like being left out of the starting line up. When Sarah came on for the first time in this match, she did not look comfortable. Sheila said to me "it's because she did not start the game, it always puts her off". Sarah then settled down, and was soon passing the ball around with great accuracy, and looking like her old self.

The supporters were loving the match, and in the crowd were the Duchess of Cambridge, and also Dame Kelly Holmes. They were cheering GB on as much as anyone.

Great Britain were playing excellent hockey, and even the players who had not performed in most of the previous matches, were playing well. Although GB has secured a number of penalty corners in the first half, they had not been able to capitalise on them.

The half time whistle went and although GB looked the more dominant force on the field, they had still not scored. I said to Sheila "we have another 35 minutes to secure the win and get the bronze medal".

The second half started and Great Britain still looked the best side. They were passing the ball well, tackling well, defending well, but they still hadn't scored. The crowd of mainly 16000 British supporters, were urging them on, encouraging them to get that 1st goal. Then in the 45th minute Alex Danson scored from a penalty corner, 1-0 to Great Britain. I have never seen a crowd of supporters so delighted, the noise was deafening.

Although GB were now 1-0 up, there was still a long way to go, and they needed to score again. New Zealand were not out of the bronze medal match yet, and they would try their damndest to win.

Sarah was still playing really well, and Sheila and I knew as always she would give everything to get this win.

Great Britain played some superb hockey, beating the New Zealand defence, and again were awarded a penalty corner, in the 59th minute.
Georgie Twigg injected the ball, and Crista Cullen struck the ball home with every ounce of power her body could muster, it was a superb goal. The crowd were once again delighted; it was now 2-0 to Great Britain
Although GB were now two goals up they could not sit back. New Zealand would always bring the game back to them.

In the 63rd minute GB were again awarded a penalty corner. The area that the penalty corner was being taken from was at the opposite end from where Sheila and I were sitting. We did not have a great view from where we were, we could see Great Britain setting up their positions, ready to take the penalty corner, but not much else. The ball was injected to Kate Walsh, who then pushed the ball out to the right hand side, a roar went up, and GB had scored again.

Sheila turned to me and said, "I think Sarah just scored the winning goal for the Olympic bronze medal".

From where I was sitting I could not see who had scored, but then it came up on the score board, and the commentator announced the scorer of the third goal as Sarah Thomas. We were overwhelmed with emotion. It had long been a dream of mine that Sarah would score the winning goal in a match for an Olympic medal.

There was still over 10 minutes of this game remaining, with Great Britain winning by 3 goals to 0. A win for New Zealand now looked out of reach, but you don't take anything for granted until that final whistle blows, and GB were not going to lose this lead.

Great Britain were still very dominant, and were keeping the now tired looking New Zealand under control.

Some uncontrolled play by GB in the circle led to New Zealand being awarded a penalty corner in the 68th minute, from which they scored it was now 3-1. Could

New Zealand put up a last gasp fight to maybe get a draw, and push GB into extra time?
With just 3 minutes to go to the end of the game, Sheila turned to me and said "Sarah has won a bronze medal". It was an amazing moment for Sheila and me. All the years of dedication, all the years of training, all the disappointments and all the time we had spent apart as a family, had now been rewarded. And if anyone deserved a medal it was Sarah.

The final whistle blew, and Great Britain had won their first Olympic medal since 1992.

Just a few days ago, after Great Britain had been beaten by Argentina, Sarah had been inconsolable. Now looking at her on the pitch with all her team mates, basking in the glory of winning an Olympic bronze medal, she was overjoyed.
I can't put into words how proud Sheila and I were at that moment, we were both crying tears of real happiness. All the parents of the players, who were sat by us, congratulated and hugged each other. As parents we had all been through a huge

roller coaster of emotions over the past two weeks.

I felt as if a huge weight had been taken off my shoulders. The relief I felt now that it was all over was immense. Sheila and I would not have to sit through another game praying for a good outcome, ever.

There was still one match to be played later in the evening at 8.00 pm. It was the gold medal match between the Netherlands and Argentina. After that game, the medal ceremony would take place.

Sheila and I watched the game, but to be honest, we were so elated with Sarah winning a medal; I don't think we cared who won.

The outcome of the game for the gold medal was that the Netherlands beat Argentina by 2-0.

We had to wait until 10.00 pm that night to watch the medal ceremony, but it was well worth it. The three teams were standing on the podium, awaiting their medals. Great Britain were first to be presented with their bronze medals, then

Argentina were presented with their silver medals and then the Netherlands were presented with their gold medals. Each team being cheered by the supporters, with Great Britain getting most of the cheers, and it was well deserved.

As each player from GB was presented with their medal, their face was shown on the big screens around the stadium. When it was Sarah's turn, to have her medal placed around her neck, the picture on the screen said it all, Sarah was beaming. And to top it all, Ann Ellis the president of Wales Hockey who was presenting the flowers to the team, stopped and gave Sarah a hug or as we call it in Wales, a "cwtch".

Great Britain Hockey had taken over a function room, at the Grange hotel near St. Pauls Cathedral. This was for the use of family and friends during the Olympic Games. On the days that we used the Grange, Sheila would always call in to St. Pauls Cathedral, to light candles for lost loved ones. Sheila also said a little prayer each time for a good outcome for Sarah. Seems, the power of prayer works.

Chapter 15

After the medal ceremony, Sheila and I made our way back to our hotel. We were absolutely exhausted; not only from the travelling, but from all the different emotions we had been through that day. Tomorrow, Saturday, was going to be another very busy day for us.

During the Olympic Games, Hyde Park had been turned into a huge concert arena. With live bands, huge screens showing different Olympic sports and food and drink stands. All of this excluding the food and drink was free of charge, and was a great way for people who could not get tickets to the Olympic Games, to join in the celebrations.

Team GB also had a VIP section in Hyde Park for all the athletes, family and friends.
This was a lovely private area where as parents we could relax with other parents and families of all the other athletes.

Again in this area we had food and drink and also large TV screens to watch the Olympics.

The plan was, that Sheila and I would make our way on Saturday morning to Hyde Park, where Team GB had their VIP family and friends meeting place. Then at about 5.30 pm the GB hockey team would be presented on the main stage at Hyde Park in front of about 40000 people, displaying their medals.

Sheila and I had a wonderful afternoon with all the other parents, chatting and laughing. Everyone was relaxed and so proud of their off springs medal winning achievement.

Word came through that the GB hockey team were backstage in the main arena, waiting to come out on stage in front of the massive crowd.

We all made our way from the Team GB area to the main park, where there was another VIP area for athlete's family and friends only. We all had a fantastic view from where we were standing. The GB hockey team filed out on to the stage, and

a massive cheer went up from the 40000 crowd.
This was another very proud moment for us, to see Sarah being congratulated, by so many people.

The team were led off stage for yet another press conference and photo shoot, before they too came to the family and friends area.
Once everyone had arrived, we toasted the team's success with a glass of champagne. For the team it was now party time. They had done their job and it was now time for them to relax and enjoy, possible one of their best moments in life.

The Grange Hotel was where the team's success was going to be celebrated. GB hockey had organised a party at the hotel for the mcn's and women's hockey squads.
Sheila and I intended to go to the party, but only for a short while. After all it was Sarah's time to enjoy herself, and we would be travelling back home to Wales early the following morning.

Sheila Sarah and I left the family and friends party to make our way to the Grange Hotel which was near St. Pauls Cathedral. We caught the tube from Knightsbridge. We had only been on the tube a few minutes when someone said "that's Sarah Thomas I watched you score the winning goal last night". The next moment, Sarah was surrounded by people wanting photos and autographs. They asked did she have her medal on her and could they see and hold it. Sarah loved every minute of showing off her medal to the people on the tube train, a moment to remember.

The party at the Grange Hotel was in full swing when we arrived. Sarah had to go and change from her Team GB tracksuit which she had to wear to Hyde Park, into her casual party clothes.
Sarah had arranged for some friends of hers to have tickets to the party. Zoe and Nick Lamb were there, as was Helen Grant a former GB hockey player and very good friend of Sarah's.

I don't know how many times Sarah had her photo taken with her medal whilst we were there, but she took it all in her stride, and loved every minute.

Sheila and I stayed at the party for just over an hour. We left about the same time as the other parents, leaving the young ones to enjoy themselves.

We gave Sarah a massive hug, again telling her how proud we were of her achievement, and that we would speak to her the following day.

Sheila and I left the Grange Hotel for the last time, and once again made our way back to our hotel. We were on as much of a high, I think, as Sarah. It's difficult to explain the immense feeling of pride and satisfaction that Sheila and I had at that time.

Chapter 16

Sunday the 12th of August 2012. The London Olympic Games was now over for us, although the closing ceremony for the

London 2012 Olympics was being held later on that night.

Sheila and I would be watching it, back home in Wales.

Back home in Wales Sheila and I were reflecting over the past two weeks. Talking about the things we liked and the things we didn't like, namely all the travelling that we had to do. But the outcome was just right and it was worth it. Sarah was now, an Olympic bronze medallist.

But could the outcome have been different?

Before the team for GB hockey was selected, there were 27 or 28 players available for selection. I had a printed list of all the players and I had ticked off the names of the players who would certainly be selected. I had put question marks against some players who would maybe get selected, and I had crossed out the names of the players who in my opinion were not up to playing in an Olympic Games. When selection was announced, I was shocked to see at least three of the players that I had crossed off my list, get selected. I firmly believe that if a different

team had been selected, Great Britain
hockey would have won the gold medal.

So that's it, an eighteen year journey
completed. Sarah has achieved her goal of
winning an Olympic medal and that is
what the journey has been all about.
As a family, we have been through hell of
a lot to make this happen. There have
been good times, bad times and really sad
times but we have all coped.
Sarah has been the one, who has had to
give up the most. Her teen years were not
like any other teen, and most of her early
adult life has not been what we would call
a normal adult life. Always training,
always travelling, and always focused on
just one thing, an Olympic medal.

We would all like to thank everyone who
has either helped us on this journey, or
who has been on the journey with us at
some point.

Cheers!

Printed in Great Britain
by Amazon.co.uk, Ltd.,
Marston Gate.